YOUR SUPER QUICK GUIDE TO LEARNING ONLINE

T0349518

Sara Miller McCune founded SAGE Publishing in 1965 to support the dissemination of usable knowledge and educate a global community. SAGE publishes more than 1000 journals and over 800 new books each year, spanning a wide range of subject areas. Our growing selection of library products includes archives, data, case studies and video. SAGE remains majority owned by our founder and after her lifetime will become owned by a charitable trust that secures the company's continued independence.

Los Angeles | London | New Delhi | Singapore | Washington DC | Melbourne

JANET E. SALMONS

YOUR SUPER QUICK GUIDE TO LEARNING ONLINE

$SAGE

Los Angeles | London | New Delhi
Singapore | Washington DC | Melbourne

Los Angeles | London | New Delhi
Singapore | Washington DC | Melbourne

SAGE Publications Ltd
1 Oliver's Yard
55 City Road
London EC1Y 1SP

SAGE Publications Inc.
2455 Teller Road
Thousand Oaks, California 91320

SAGE Publications India Pvt Ltd
B 1/I 1 Mohan Cooperative Industrial Area
Mathura Road
New Delhi 110 044

SAGE Publications Asia-Pacific Pte Ltd
3 Church Street
#10-04 Samsung Hub
Singapore 049483

Editor: Jai Seaman
Assistant editor: Lauren Jacobs
Production editor: Ian Antcliff
Marketing manager: Catherine Slinn
Cover design: Shaun Mercier
Typeset by: C&M Digitals (P) Ltd, Chennai, India

**Library of Congress Control Number:
Available**

British Library Cataloguing in Publication data

A catalogue record for this book is available from
the British Library

ISBN 978-1-5297-5440-7
ISBN 978-1-5297-5439-1 (pbk)

At SAGE we take sustainability seriously. Most of our products are printed in the UK using responsibly
sourced papers and boards. When we print overseas we ensure sustainable papers are used as
measured by the PREPS grading system. We undertake an annual audit to monitor our sustainability.

CONTENTS

ABOUT THE AUTHOR

Janet Salmons is a passionate educator. She spent 18 years teaching and guiding Masters and doctoral students online at Capella University. She currently teaches adults online through the Boulder Lifelong Learning program and other organizations. She has consulted with universities about online course design, and worked with faculty to improve online instruction. She is a frequent presenter about e-learning.

Dr. Salmons is a free-range scholar, writer, coach, and artist through her business, Vision2Lead. She serves as the Methods Guru for SAGE Publications' research community, www.MethodSpace.com. Areas of interest include emerging research methods, as well as teaching and collaborative learning in the digital age. Her most recent books are: *Reframing and Rethinking Collaboration in Higher Education and Beyond: A Practical Guide for Doctoral Students and Early Career Researchers* with Narelle Lemon (2020), *Publishing from your Doctoral Research: Create and Use a Publication Strategy* with Helen Kara (2020), *What Kind of Researcher Are You?* (2020), *Learning to Collaborate, Collaborating to Learn* (2019), *Find the Theory in Your Research* (2019), *Getting Data Online* (2019), and *Doing Qualitative Research Online* (2016). She is an honorary member of the Textbook and Academic Authors Association Council of Fellows (2019) and received the Mike Keedy Award (2018) in recognition of enduring service to authors. She lives and works in Boulder, Colorado.

INTRODUCTION

Welcome to online learning! It is the same, but different, from face-to-face learning. It is the same in terms of the tasks of reading course materials, writing papers, and completing assignments being familiar. But it is different because some or all of your interactions are mediated by electronic communications. It is at once more flexible, allowing you to study at your convenience, and more demanding, because you must have the discipline to work more independently. You still have discussions and team projects, but you communicate and coordinate your work online. This means that online learning requires the same study skills you need face-to-face, in addition to technology skills, online communication skills, and time-management skills. This book is designed to help you understand the expectations for your online course, and develop the skills you need to meet them.

If I can do it, so can you! After I earned a bachelors degree on the beautiful campus of Cornell University, I completed both my Masters and doctoral degrees in low-residency programmes that involved working with the faculty and fellow students at a distance. I went from an intensive, personal style of teaching and learning face-to-face with diverse students and respected faculty to sitting alone at my desk, trying to figure out what I was supposed to do. Yes, it was hard. But I did it, and so can you!

As luck would have it, I had the opportunity to experience distance education on the other side of the monitor, as a faculty member. I was an early adopter of e-learning, starting in 1999 to teach in one of the first institutions in the

United States to offer Masters and doctoral degrees online. I taught students who might not have otherwise been able to get a degree, because they were working, had families, or were deployed in the military. I had a chance to work closely with both faculty and students, and in the process gained an understanding about what it takes to succeed in an online milieu. While being able to use digital tools is fundamental, more important are connections with professors and peers. Respect, honesty, kindness and patience will go a long way towards making this a meaningful learning experience.

I've tried to share the lessons I learned in this book, and it is my sincere hope that you find it beneficial.

Janet Salmons, Ph.D.
Boulder, Colorado USA

WHAT IS ONLINE LEARNING AND HOW CAN I SUCCEED?

CHAPTER 1

Today's online learning builds on a history of instruction from afar, and many learners have completed academic degrees with little or no time in a physical classroom. There are several ways e-learning is offered, including hybrid classes with some face-to-face time. However, it takes a different kind of preparation, motivation, discipline and management on the part of the learner. This chapter will help you get started, and after you work through this book you will be ready to succeed in online learning.

INTRODUCTION

Online learning might seem new, but it builds on efforts to teach across distances that began in the 1800s. Remote learning is a time-tested way to make academic progress, but there is not a uniform way that institutions deliver instruction from afar. One of the first steps to take is to identify the kind of academic programme you are in, so you can prepare and manage the learning experience.

There are many ways to learn remotely!

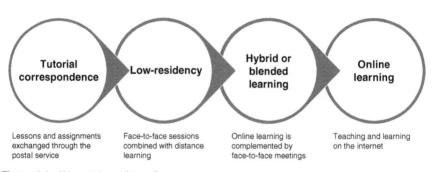

Figure 1.1   Ways to learn from afar

People started learning outside of the physical classroom setting long before the internet was invented. Distance learning programmes relied on the postal service, with learners and faculty members sending lessons and assignments back and forth. These programmes involved close tutorial relationships between faculty members and learners, often functioning on a one-to-one basis. Broadcast courses associated with public universities took advantage of the television and/ or radio. Low residency programmes mixed short-term sessions on campuses or other locations, combined with telephone consultations and correspondence. This option allowed for more student-to-student interaction than the correspondence-only programmes.

Even with the advent of the internet, these approaches are still common. With the internet, e-learning was born. Some academic programmes began to operate entirely online, with libraries, administrative services, and all support functions available to learners through digital channels. Others mix online interactions with time physically together in a bricks-and-mortar classroom, a style known as hybrid or blended learning programmes. Low-residency programmes have also continued into the internet era, with long weekend or weeklong residencies scheduled at strategic points in the term or programme. Low-residency programmes are particularly valuable where learners are geographically dispersed.

Most online classes are similar to what you would expect in your higher education experience: there is a professor and a group of students. In very large classes a tutor or teaching assistant assists the professor and runs small-group discussions. Another online trend is what are called massively open online courses, or MOOCs. These courses include recorded lectures and reading materials, with checkpoints such as quizzes. MOOCs are typically designed for independent, self-paced learning, but can be a part of your institution's offerings. Sometimes MOOCs are offered to help with skills building, remedial work, or to introduce foundations on a topic.

Remote learning has continued to grow and evolve. Success strategies vary according to the type of instruction and expectations for learners. Before strategizing about how you can learn from afar, identify the type of online learning programme you are enrolled in now or are considering. Given what you know about how your programme is organized, use this checklist to identify which of these features is included:

All learning activities are online. ☐

Some learning activities are online, some are on-campus for face-to-face class meetings or residencies. ☐

I will have a one-to-one tutorial relationship with a professor or tutor. ☐

I will be in a course with a professor and fellow students. ☐

I will have some skills-building modules. ☐

What type of remote learning will you be using?

Once you understand the type of online learning your institution or programme offers, you can find the best way to move forward.

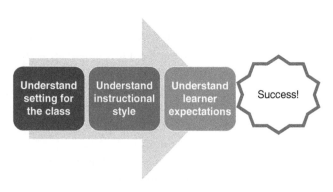

Figure 1.2 Preparing to learn online

WHAT IS THE SETTING FOR YOUR ONLINE COURSE?

When e-learning was adopted as a legitimate part of college and university curricula, the question arose: where can classes meet? Platforms known as *Learning Management Systems* (LMS) or *Virtual Learning Environments* (VLE) were developed for instructional purposes. (For simplicity, we will use the term LMS in this book.) LMS platforms provide a private online classroom space for each course. Not every institution utilizes an LMS; it is possible that your professor will use other online tools to communicate with the class.

Learning in an LMS

The LMS classroom is accessible only to those registered for the class. An LMS allows for privacy and is a safe space for discussion without the risks and distractions of the public web. The LMS is the hub for all aspects of the online course. The syllabus, readings, media, overviews or lectures from the professor, and assignments are posted in the LMS. Direct links to the library and other resources are embedded in course materials.

Web conferencing options are often integrated into the platform, so presentations or meetings involving professors and learners can take place. Threaded discussion forums allow for written responses to questions and

A student told us

'The first time I went into the LMS classroom I had a hard time navigating the space. After taking a couple of classes I am more familiar with it, but I still like to log in before the course start date and make sure I know how to find everything I need.'

comments to peers. Some LMS sites provide spaces for learners to collaborate on team projects or small-group activities. Electronic gradebooks are visible to learners so they can track progress during the semester. With the advent of the LMS, a class experience with active faculty and peer interactions became possible in ways that were not previously feasible in the one-to-one or small group distance learning of the past.

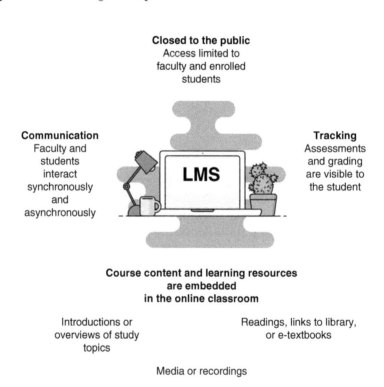

Closed to the public
Access limited to
faculty and enrolled
students

Communication
Faculty and
students
interact
synchronously
and
asynchronously

LMS

Tracking
Assessments
and grading
are visible to
the student

**Course content and learning resources
are embedded
in the online classroom**

Introductions or
overviews of study
topics

Readings, links to library,
or e-textbooks

Media or recordings

Figure 1.3 Learning Management System

e-learning with online tools

While most formal online academic programmes adopt an LMS platform, some operate on the public web or in various proprietary or open access platforms.

Presentations or discussions occur using web conferencing or using a forum app. Wikis – websites that subscribed users can add to and edit – are sometimes used for group work. Assignments are submitted by email or shared folders. The professor might specify the main communication channel as an email list or other digital tool.

The tools mentioned above have one thing in common: privacy. The exchanges between students and faculty are closed to the outside world. However, professors online can interact in public, on social media. Your professor might set up a group on a social media site, or use a hashtag to convey announcements or manage a conversation. For example, your class might engage in live micro-blogging during a major event, or your class might follow and discuss experts in your field.

Some communication is visible to the public
Access may or may not be limited to
faculty and enrolled students

Communication
Faculty and
students
interact
using email and
web conferencing,
wikis,
or social media

Digital Tools

Tracking
Assessments
and grading
are conveyed
by email or in
shared folders

**Course content and learning resources
are sent by email, posted in shared folders or wikis**

Introductions or
overviews of study
topics

Readings, links to library,
or e-textbooks

Media or recordings

Figure 1.4   Course delivery on the web

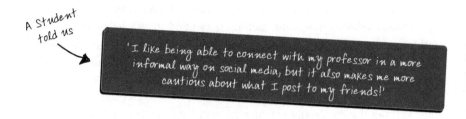

A Student told us

'I like being able to connect with my professor in a more informal way on social media, but it also makes me more cautious about what I post to my friends!'

What will I need to use the course technologies?

After looking at the Learning Management System or the combination of digital tools you expect to use, determine what you will need to participate. Here are some possibilities:

A laptop or desktop that has an operating system and memory adequate for accessing and playing online presentations or media. ❏

A web camera and microphone for participating in web conferences. A headset is preferable since it screens out background noise. ❏

A stable broadband internet connection. ❏

You will most likely need Microsoft Office, including PowerPoint and MS Word, or a comparable software suite. ❏

A quiet, comfortable learning space. ❏

See Chapter 7 for a more detailed description of technology tools and software.

IS INTERACTION SYNCHRONOUS AND/OR ASYNCHRONOUS?

Online learning relies on online communications. Approaches to communications differ, so this is another factor to evaluate when you begin a new course.

Think about the ways you communicate with family members and friends. When do you chat in real time, and when do you post a message and expect them to respond when they see it and have time to respond? To chat online in real time, we need to be simultaneously logged into the same software platform or application. We call that *synchronous communications*. When we post a message or send an email for later response, we are using *asynchronous communication*.

We can refine these terms better to describe how we use technology today. When we are online at the same time, fully focused on the exchange, we can describe that as *synchronicity*. When we are not online at the same time, but expect a response soon, we can call that *near-synchronous*. Since these forms of communication are somewhat fluid, they are shown here on a continuum (Figure 1.5).

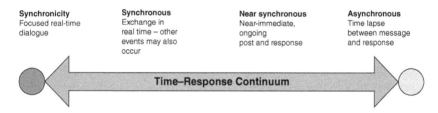

Synchronicity
Focused real-time dialogue

Synchronous
Exchange in real time – other events may also occur

Near synchronous
Near-immediate, ongoing post and response

Asynchronous
Time lapse between message and response

Time–Response Continuum

Figure 1.5 Time–response continuum

e-learning activities can use any of these forms of communication, so it is important to understand the distinctions and related expectations. Some academic institutions want to include learners from diverse time zones across the country or the world, so they focus primarily on communication at the asynchronous side of the continuum. This means presentations or lectures are recorded and posted. Discussions involve posting responses or comments in the LMS, class forum, or another digital tool. Questions to your professor might be posed by email. Some professors in primarily asynchronous learning environments hold office hours when you can log in to discuss any issues. Faculty can also offer appointments for private coaching, supervision, or other one-to-one consultations.

Other institutions emphasize synchronous communications, in which courses focus on communications at the synchronous end of the continuum.

This means the professor gives lectures and students have regular meetings in a web conferencing platform. Learners use asynchronous modes for completing papers or assignments.

Specific practices and skills-building to improve communications with your professor and fellow students will be discussed in forthcoming chapters. For now, use Table 1.1, below, to make notes on the type(s) of communication used in your online course.

WHAT IS YOUR PROFESSOR'S INSTRUCTIONAL STYLE?

Professors adapt their teaching styles to the online environment – and learners must adapt along with them! Some decisions about how to go about teaching their classes are up to them, while others are made by the institution or department. If the institution or department has an established instructional style, you can assume that each course will be taught in a similar way even though you have a different professor. In situations where it is up to the professor, each course could be taught in a different way.

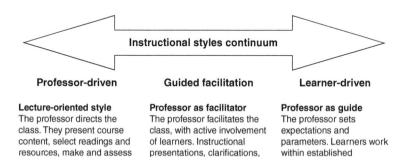

Professor-driven	Guided facilitation	Learner-driven
Lecture-oriented style The professor directs the class. They present course content, select readings and resources, make and assess assignments and papers. Communication is centred around clarifications or questions about the content presented by the professor.	**Professor as facilitator** The professor facilitates the class, with active involvement of learners. Instructional presentations, clarifications, or examples are offered when needed. They assign core readings, point students toward other relevant resources.	**Professor as guide** The professor sets expectations and parameters. Learners work within established frameworks, and are responsible for finding and creating learning activities and resources.

Figure 1.6 Instructional styles

You can find three main teaching styles online. We will call them *professor-driven*, *guided facilitation*, and *learner-driven*. Some courses might use one, others might use a combination of styles.

As you can see, your roles and responsibilities are very different, depending on the degree to which the professor takes charge or expects learners to be self-directed. You can anticipate that a course that is professor-driven, lecture-oriented, is going to be low-touch. The class size is probably larger, and typically learners have fewer opportunities for one-to-one coaching. You might have tutors or teaching assistants in discussion leader roles, who can also answer your questions.

If you find that you are in a facilitated course, you need to be clear about what is up to learners to decide, and what parts of the course the professor will lead. A facilitative professor who is committed to guiding and mentoring will have a high-touch style. That is, they know the students personally, in a way not possible in a large lecture course. You might have a relationship with the professor, and be able to discuss not only course content, but also academic or career planning.

If you are in a learner-driven course, where students have a lot of flexibility to determine their goals and activities, you will need to be prepared to take more responsibility for your own work. If peer-to-peer collaboration is central to the course, you will need to think about how you will work with others virtually.

You might encounter more than one style of instruction in a given course. You might have some lectures, either live or recorded, as well as group projects. Look at the syllabus to see what is required and look at the class size. Those two pieces of information will help you understand the kinds of activities you will need to master to complete the course with high marks.

When you understand the instructional style(s) for the course you are taking, you will be better prepared to meet the expectations. In coming chapters you will have a chance to develop the tactics that will work best in your own learning situation. For now, note what you know about the instructional style that is (or will be) used in your online learning class, using Table 1.1.

Table 1.1   Identifying the types and technologies for online learning

Factor	My course(s)	Technologies: communication tools or platforms	Notes
All-online or hybrid			
LMS or combination of digital tools			
Synchronous and/or asynchronous			
High-touch or low-touch instructional styles			
Other factors specific to your programme			
Other factors specific to your programme			

Learn to succeed in courses with any combination of online factors!

You can use and expand on your notes from Table 1.1 when you move forward in this book! You will look at what each factor means to you, given your own goals and preferred way to engage with your studies. You will look at how you can get the most out of each online course so you are ready to advance to the next stage of your academic programme, or apply what you have learned in your professional life.

HOW DO I GET READY FOR ONLINE LEARNING?

A student told us

'Without a set class meeting schedule, it can be hard to stay focused and make the best use of my time.'

Setting goals and objectives

How can you achieve your goals unless you know what they are? The first step to achieving your goals is articulating them. Sometimes just writing goals down helps to establish them in your mind. When you're writing your 'want to achieve list' make sure you set goals you can achieve in this academic term. If the goals this term fit with larger educational goals, indicate the general timeframe. To begin with, think about these questions:

- What do you want to achieve in this course?
- Do you want to gain knowledge of your topic of study, so you can move into advanced coursework?
- Do you want to delve into the literature in this field?
- Do you want to gain skills you can apply professionally?
- Do you want to network with others and find study partners or people who might be co-researchers or co-authors in the future?
- Do you want to prove to yourself and others that you can complete this level of academic work?
- Do you want to improve your digital literacy and learn online research, communication, and collaboration skills from learning online?

Try to include goals in your list that are SMART. That way, you'll be able to tick things off your list and feel like you've achieved something. Setting SMART goals is a recognized method to help you define what it is you want to achieve, and for reflecting on how you can achieve it in a timely manner.

SMART stands for:

- Specific
- Measurable
- Achievable
- Relevant
- Time-bound

Use the following table to identify at least three main SMART goals you would like to achieve while learning online. Identify one goal related to course content, one goal related to your use of technology, and one personal goal.

Table 1.2   SMART goals

Specific: Goal description / title	Measurable: How will you know when you have achieved it?	Achievable: Can you honestly achieve this goal? Yes or No	Relevant: Detail how you will achieve this goal	Time-bound: Set a date for achieving each goal: this term or long-term
Course content				
Use of technology				
Personal goals				

Using the Pomodoro Technique to meet academic goals

Sometimes getting focused and staying focused are the primary stumbling blocks to achieving our goals. A technique many students use is called the *Pomodoro Technique*. Pomodoro is the Italian word for tomato, and the technique is named this simply because the timer used by Francesco Cirillo, who created this technique, was in the shape of a tomato. Really you can use any timer you choose, you can use a stopwatch or any clock with an alarm, but do not use your phone. If you use your phone, you may be distracted by a text or a message and this technique is all about maintaining focus and actually working when you are supposed to be working.

There are five steps in the Pomodoro Technique and it really does help to focus your mind and get the work done. Steps in the Pomodoro method:

1   **Decide on task** Decide what task you're going to work on.
2   **Set timer** Set a timer for 25 minutes.

3   **Work on task** Work on the task until the timer rings.

4   **Take a short break** Take a short break of only five minutes, then return to step 2.

5   **Repeat four times** and then **take a longer break of 15–30 minutes**.

You can complete these steps as often as you need until you have completed your task.

If you use the Pomodoro Technique every day or even just three times a week, you will be astonished at how much you manage to achieve in a very small space of time.

Reflecting and evaluating

If you find that you don't have enough time to complete all the tasks you need to, or you're spending too long on certain tasks at the expense of others, stop and reflect on what you need to do to achieve your goals. Reflecting on and evaluating the way you manage your time can make a real difference to your productivity, effectiveness and health and well-being.

Questions to help you reflect on and evaluate the way you manage your time:

- Did you get through everything you needed to do today? If so, did you use any particular strategies to ensure you stayed on target?
- Did you prioritize your tasks for the day?
- Do you know how much time you spent on the different tasks you carried out today?
- Were you surprised by the amount of time a task took to complete?
- Did you plan your day, or did you go with the flow?
- Have you noticed any time-management strategies that *didn't* work for you?

Review your answers. They should give you some easy wins to improve your time management – for example, if you planned your day today and you don't normally, but it helped you get through all your tasks, you can start to make more use of this in the future.

Prepare to manage your time and keep your study–work–life in balance

Studying online means you have to set your own hours. On the one hand, studying online is more flexible, because you can choose when to complete the asynchronous parts of the coursework. On the other hand, without the structure you have when you must appear in a physical classroom at a given time, it is easy to let things slide. Start now to set your own time management framework.

While you might have some synchronous sessions, you are responsible for scheduling much of your work. Additional time might be needed during the transition, particularly while you learn to adapt to online learning. Consistently working increased hours has a cumulative effect and can cause damage to your mental health.

Studying for long hours isn't always the most productive, or effective, use of your time. You might be better studying for a couple of hours and then taking a break to give you time to recharge, before going back to your books.

Remember that 'me-time' is incredibly important. This is time that we all need to think, relax, exercise and recharge our batteries. You've worked for this time, so don't feel guilty about taking it. Also, if you don't give yourself some 'guilt-free me-time' to recharge your batteries, then how will you have enough energy to complete the tasks you need to complete? When planning your time, schedule in downtime from work or study. Don't forget to sleep! Find more on self-care in Chapter 7.

Don't let stress get you down

Adapting to a new learning environment with unfamiliar norms can be stressful. Make sure to take care of yourself so you can feel relaxed and ready to do your best. Here are some stress-reduction tips:

- **Learn to breathe** Breathe slowly and deeply from the abdomen.

- **Take more exercise** Sport releases endorphins, which creates a feeling of well-being, and regular exercise helps regulate breathing, as well as providing time for reflection and thought. Don't overdo it though. Pay attention to your body's limits.

- **Talk to someone** Rather than bottling your problems up, share them with friends, housemates, family, tutors, a counsellor, or whoever you feel comfortable trusting and talking to.

- **Write it down** Keeping a private and securely protected diary or journal can help relieve stress, help you put things into perspective, and allows you to be open and honestly reflective.

- **Be creative** Sketching, painting, art journaling, playing music do more than give you a break. Creative thinking is essential to academic life, so play can help your work!

- **Make time for yourself** Make use of time-management strategies to ensure you have time to relax and unwind without feeling guilty about tasks or assignments you need to complete or other people you want to help.

- **Meditate** This involves learning techniques for relaxation. See if a local group is teaching meditation or mindfulness techniques.

- **Learn a relaxation technique** You can teach yourself to relax with the help of relaxation media, apps and books.

- **Visualization** This involves picturing and recording how we think things will realistically happen. Visualizing yourself handling a situation better can give you psychological experience for when the real situation happens.

CHECKLIST FOR ONLINE LEARNING PREPARATION

I have identified the type of online learning approach the course will use. ❑

I know whether I will need to log-in once to a Learning Management System, or need to access multiple digital tools. ❑

I understand the primary communication mode for the course, synchronous or asynchronous. ❑

I have identified the instructional style of the professor. ❑

I set goals for this course, and for my academic programme as a whole. ❑

I thought about how I will keep balanced and manage my time. ❑

I reflected on ways to reduce stress so I can do my best work. ❑

 Getting started

How do I communicate electronically?

To think through communication technology choices you might make when learning online, look more closely at the ones you typically use for your own personal and social communications. Keep a communications log for three days. Note what form(s) of communication you use, with whom (family member, friend, or university/work). Indicate whether you used synchronous, asynchronous, or a combination of modes to communicate. Reflect on what was effective and met your needs, for what tasks or activities. Why?

Table 1.3   Communications log

Day	Friend/family or school-related	Communications technology	Synchronous/ asynchronous	Thoughts and observations
1				
2				
3				

2 What kinds of learning experiences do I like?

Reflect on your previous face-to-face classes. What kinds of activities did you feel were the best learning experiences for you? Which did not work well for you? Why?

Lectures	☐	Textbooks	☐
Guest speakers	☐	Short assignments	☐
Media	☐	Class discussions	☐
Podcasts	☐	Research papers	☐
Library research	☐	Research projects	☐
Articles	☐	Field or service projects	☐

Other ....

Based on this exercise, how would you describe your preferences?

....

....

....

Do you learn best when you work and study alone or with a group?

....

....

....

Given the choice, what learning activities do you want in your online class?

....

....

....

3 Try the Pomodoro Technique

Choose a non-academic task, and practise timing your work time and breaks. Is this a technique you can use? Why? If not, how can you adapt this model to better fit your habits and work styles?

HOW DO I GET THE MOST FROM DIFFERENT TYPES OF INSTRUCTION?

CHAPTER 2

60 second summary

Online teaching and learning can take many forms and success combines self-awareness, understanding of the course structure and instructional modes, and respect for your professor. In this chapter we will explore some common options: learning styles, thinking and working processes, and instructional modes. We will look at ways to prepare for and engage with learning activities in online classes. Note that in coming chapters we will dig deeply into reading assignments (Chapter 3), written assignments (Chapter 4), and group assignments (Chapter 5).

INTRODUCTION: LEARNING STYLES

Before you can decide how to navigate your current online or hybrid course(s), take a few minutes to reflect on your learning style(s). Once you are clear about what works best for you, you'll be able to find the best tactics for success in the course, whether or not it was designed with your learning style in mind. When you prepare for the synchronous and/or asynchronous modes of instruction and interactions, you will feel more confident about learning the content of the course.

First, think about how you learn best

Educational researchers have studied the ways children and adults learn since long before we used technology for these purposes, and researchers have studied online learning as well. Naturally, there are many theories and piles of articles on the subject. Let's look at the practical implications of a couple of theories and what they mean for you. The first is about how you prefer to access information, and the second is about how you proceed with an assignment, and your on- and offline study habits.

You may have been exposed to the idea that while we all receive information in different ways, we each respond more deeply with one or more of those ways. One person loves reading, another thinks it is boring. One tunes out audio, another leans in. One finds images memorable; another forgets it by lunch time. One needs to touch or move, and another prefers a static study space. These possibilities align with a model called VARK (Fleming and Mills, 1992):

- **V**isual learners prefer to see information represented as images.
- **A**uditory learners prefer to hear information.
- **R**eading/**W**riting learners prefer information to be displayed as words.
- **K**inesthetic learners prefer to touch, feel, or move.

To more specifically describe how we access and interact with information online, let's expand this model and look at the types of materials associated with each preference:

- **V**isual: Photographs, graphics and graphic books, infographics, diagrams, data visualizations, drawings or artwork, mind maps or geographic maps, GIFs
- **A**uditory: Podcasts, recordings, music, lectures, audio-only calls using voice over the internet or the telephone
- **A**udio-Visual: Media, webinars, web conferencing, video chats
- **R**eading: Online with websites, blogs, and social media posts, and/or offline with downloaded articles and eBooks
- **W**riting: Online with text chats or posts, email, comments, reviews to peer learners and/or offline with essays or papers, journaling
- **K**inesthetic: Studying with a standing desk, practical applications of ideas, fieldwork, moving or walking while listening or observing
- **O**ffline-analog: Working in a laboratory, using analog tools for journaling, notetaking, or drafting written or visual responses.

VAARWKO is not a catchy acronym, but it offers a more expansive way to think about ways we interact with information. Given today's technologies, it makes sense to add audiovisual resources to the list. And given that we use mobile technologies, moving with *kinesthetic* learning can include a wider range of possibilities. No matter what is presented online, we still need to complete some learning activities offline or in-person.

Figure 2.1   Learning styles

Take a moment to think about the times you have most enjoyed accessing educational materials, or times when you have felt bored, distracted, or unable to grasp the ideas being presented. Do you have a primary learning style? A second choice? Are there any that do not work for you at all?

 What is your learning style?

Think about the times when you felt truly engaged, and when you connected with the learning activities in a course, or in a non-academic setting. Was the information presented to you in visual, auditory, written, or physical form? Or was it a mix? What did you do with that information: create visuals, spoken presentations, written papers, or kinesthetic experiences? Record examples and note ways you have connected online or mixed on- and offline for each one.

Table 2.1 My learning styles

My primary, secondary, non-working learning styles	Examples of when you have used this style	Ways in which you have connected with this style online	How effective was this style for you?
Visual			
Auditory			
Audiovisual			
Reading			
Writing			
Kinesthetic			
Offline-analog			
Mix of _____ & _____			
Mix of _____ & _____			

Finding course materials that fit your style

Look at the materials and activities assigned for your current course(s). How would you categorize them? To what extent do the materials correspond to your preferred style? If they do not, here are some suggestions for finding related materials and/or adapting them to meet your style(s):

- **Looking for more aural or audiovisual materials?** Many textbooks include audio recordings or videos in the supplementary resources. Look on the publisher's book site, and on the author's book site. You can also look on video archives, or on YouTube for recorded talks by the textbook author or other experts on the subject. Look for podcasts on the subject. If your library subscribes to SAGE Research Methods, you can find a collection of videos and podcasts by researchers.

- **Looking for ways to balance kinesthetic movement with sedentary studies?** In addition to a standing desk that allows you to avoid long periods of sitting, consider putting audio content on a mobile device and listening while you walk, run, or exercise.

- **Looking for ways to balance analog and digital?** After watching or reading materials or events online, put ideas into your own words in a physical journal, or express them in a drawing, mind map, or diagram.

One option would be to ask your professor for suggestions about how to best align your course experience and your learning styles. If they know, for example, that learners prefer audiovisual materials, they might record assignment instructions or feedback rather than write it. (Later in this chapter we will look at ways to communicate with your professor.)

Expanding your mindset to appreciate all styles

Some Learning Management Systems seem most conducive to learning activities that focus on reading written materials and posting written responses, but increasingly, visual materials and exchanges are central to online learning. Your online course might focus heavily on one style or another, but it is best to be prepared for all forms of information and interaction. We shouldn't limit ourselves to the styles that might come most easily to us. At the same time, if we understand our styles, we can build a comprehensive approach that will help us make the best of the online learning environment and instructional style.

ACTIVITY Strengthening my working styles

Go back to your learning styles table. Ask yourself:

Are there types of information or types of interactions you find challenging?

....

....

....

....

What can you do to improve your ability to learn using all types?

....

....

....

....

NEXT, THINK ABOUT HOW YOU APPROACH COURSEWORK

Do you resonate with any of these descriptions?

- You see what is due this term and carefully plan the steps for completing each deliverable.
- You see what is due this week (or maybe tomorrow!) and get the work done as the clock is ticking for submission without penalty.

You have probably developed a system for approaching assignments that you have used to get to this point in your schooling. Your existing system may or may not work well in an online environment. For one thing, online you have more flexibility but also more responsibility for your work. Assignments often stretch over multiple weeks or learning units of the term. If you fall behind in an online class, it can be difficult or impossible to catch up. (See Chapter 1 for more on time management.)

Thought processes and learning

Let's look at and adapt another educational theory in a way that can help you identify your current system and improve the process you can use for tackling online coursework. Ivana Šimonová and colleagues (Šimonová et al., 2011; Šimonová et al., 2020) updated the thinking of an earlier scholar (Johnston, 2006). Johnston thought that students combine one of four types of processes when working on assignments:

- **Sequential processors** want clear directions so they can plan their work step-by-step.

- **Precise processors** are detail-oriented and look for all the information they need before moving forward.

- **Confluent processors** take a holistic approach. They are creative imaginers and unique presenters.

- **Technical processors** are hands-on builders and independent thinkers.

Let's add one more, the social processor.

- **Social processors** find meaning in interactions and collaborative efforts with others.

Let's look at how these styles might play out in a research paper assignment due at the end of the term.

- If you are a *sequential processor*, you want to have the requirements at hand, and divide larger assignments like this into discrete parts before devising a plan and timeline. You might create an outline, then look for the articles you want to analyse, and fill in your outline with key points and quotes, before starting to craft paragraphs for the first draft. You will identify what needs to be completed each week of the term, assemble the paper with time to proofread before submission. Your challenge is to avoid getting hung up in the process, with inadequate attention to deep reading.

- If you are a *precise processor* you might dig into the research on the topic, finding detailed information that you will put together as you move forward. Your challenge is to avoid getting bogged down in minutiae and losing track of the big picture.

- As a direct opposite, if you are a *confluent* processor, you want to visualize the big picture before breaking them down into parts to complete. You might assemble a large collection of research before trying to identify themes you can use to support your main points. Your challenge is to follow formats and styles that might seem trivial and narrow down the paper to fit within the scope of the course.

- If you are a *technical processor*, you want to use logical tactics, and demonstrate how the ideas can be applied. You do the research, honing in on ways the issue might play out in the real world. Your challenge is to integrate abstract ideas and theories with practical solutions.

- If you are a *social processor*, you want opportunities to talk with others about the ideas, and time to ask questions of those with experiences in the topics at hand.

There are advantages and disadvantages of each kind of thought and work processing. The concept of building a paper might appeal to a technical processor. A sequencing processor might be on time but have missed thinking creatively. A precise processor might find it hard to write an abstract before having details from the literature, while a confluent processor might find it hard to come up with the specific focus of the paper without seeing a holistic view of the problem. Becoming aware of your own habits and patterns will help you build on your strengths and shore up areas where your natural style will not be successful given the course requirements and protocols.

 **What is my processing approach?**

Complete the following statements to help reflect on your processing approach.

Based on the thought-processing descriptions, my dominant processing approach is: ....

I mix these approaches: ....

My approach is:

a   consistent

b   situational

Advantages I can build on in an online class: ....

I need to work on: ....

Adapting thought processing for online learning

The biggest challenge is to align your learning and processing styles to the professor's style and the online course framework. You will discover that many online courses are designed for sequential completion of a series of learning activities. Learning activities are associated with a week of the course or learning unit (which could cross more than one week). A large research paper is typically submitted in incremental steps, with deliverables submitted throughout the term. For example:

- Paper concept or abstract
- Outline
- Annotated bibliography
- First draft
- Final draft.

A collaborative project might have deliverables such as:

- Problem statement for the project
- Team charter or agreement
- First draft
- Team process check-in
- Final project or presentation.

Learn more about reading course materials in Chapter 3, writing in Chapter 4, and peer collaboration in Chapter 5.

Naturally, you will use other forms of processing within the sequential arrangement of steps. You might use confluent thinking to imagine the purpose for the paper or project, precise thinking to identify details within each step, and technical thinking to make sure the steps will build toward the desired conclusion.

Multi-week papers and projects are organized this way for two inter-related reasons: 1) your professor wants to make sure that you are making progress and staying within the parameters of the assignment; and 2) the professor does not want you to get off track and be unable to complete the course successfully. The professor's interest in your completion of the course might be reflected in the grading protocols. It is not unusual to see policies as outlined below.

I expect that you will follow the timeline for the course. If you have special circumstances, please contact me. While assignments can be posted after the due date, points will be deducted.

- Posted on time = Maximum 100% of assignment grade points.
- Two to three days past due date = Maximum 90% of grade points
- Four to six days posting later than assignment due date = Maximum 75% of grade points
- Greater than seven days posting later than assignment due date = zero grade points unless you have permission from the professor.

As you can see, this kind of policy incentivizes you to either get the assignments done or see an impact on your final marks. (Learn more about assessment in Chapter 6.)

A student told us

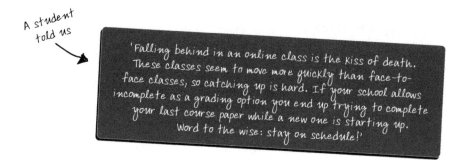

'Falling behind in an online class is the kiss of death. These classes seem to move more quickly than face-to-face classes, so catching up is hard. If your school allows incomplete as a grading option you end up trying to complete your last course paper while a new one is starting up. Word to the wise: stay on schedule!'

In some institutions, each course is structured differently, and depends on each professor's teaching methods. This allows flexibility for more courses about more theoretical, conceptual, or literary topics to be taught differently from courses that are more procedural. Other academic programmes use a consistent structure across all courses. In such programmes, once you internalize a process that works – whether or not it is the process that comes naturally – you can use it in every course. The student who examines the syllabus and course documents to identify how it is organized will thrive online.

ONLINE COMMUNICATION AND INSTRUCTION

You are accustomed to communicating electronically, so many of the ways you'll interact in an online class will be familiar to you. You are probably accustomed to a face-to-face classroom, so modes of instruction will be familiar to you. The difference comes in how online professors use electronic communications in one or more modes of instruction. In Chapter 1 you identified your class setting and basic characteristics about how it is organized. Let's look at how to work with them.

Higher education courses are typically differentiated by style and class size. Lecture courses are large, so one professor can instruct a large class of students. You most likely have little interaction with those professors, working more closely with tutors or teaching assistants. Seminar courses are quite different: class size is small, and students interact intensely with the professor and each other. Certain courses have an experiential component, such as a laboratory, a service-learning or field project, or with games, debates, or role plays. Courses might be based around self-paced learning or projects that involve little interaction with professor or learners.

Similarly, online courses can be professor-driven with lectures or presentations as the main event and a large class size. They can also be experiential or discussion-based, with professors as facilitators and a class size that allows for students to get acquainted and learn together.

Relating to your online professor

It goes without saying that your online professor is your partner in success. They hold the power of the pen – the marking pen. If you do not have a shared sense of purpose, and a common interpretation of expectations, problems can arise.

Online professors will generally spell out the roles they will take in the class. They will define their availability for consultations and their preferred modes of communication. Make note of this guidance and follow it. If it is missing, ask.

As in any situation, professors have personalities, preferences, and ways they fulfill teaching roles. A more social-processing oriented professor might establish a learning community with lots of dialogue, while a precise-processor might be more interested in getting assignments submitted and marked. The way the professor introduces the course and their expectations will probably signal some clues about their style(s).

There is a balancing act at play in online education. Online professors typically teach multiple courses and have many students to follow. Much of the work is submitted in writing. Whereas a face-to-face discussion might involve listening to and facilitating the group for an hour, an online discussion that occurs in writing generates many posts and responses that require much more time to read. Nevertheless, they are committed to your success and are concerned about your performance.

Respecting your professor's time is of the utmost importance. If you make an appointment because you have a problem or question, be punctual. Come prepared. If you are communicating by email, be specific about what you are asking. If you want them to read something prior to a meeting, provide it as far in advance as possible and note your question or point where you need feedback.

If you are in a class where the professor has regular one-to-one or small-group meetings, keep track of your interactions with your professor, so when you meet with them again you can demonstrate that you have addressed any recommendations. If you are taking more than one course, create a contact log for each one. (See Table 2.2). This kind of contact log will be a good reference point if you have questions or issues about the final marks for your course.

Table 2.2   Professor contact log

Date	Assignment or project	Main topics discussed	Comments	Action steps and timeline

On the personal side

You might have a non-academic issue, such as a health problem, that you want to discuss privately. Let them know what it is that you need, and ask for the best way to communicate about it.

While respect for your professor is an underpinning for your relationship, this should be mutual. If your professor is not answering emails, not reviewing work, or is not posting to the online discussion, contact them. In one memorable experience an online professor was on vacation out of the country, had an accident and was hospitalized. They had no family members to contact the university, so no one knew they were gone. For several weeks students just thought the professor was busy and didn't say anything. Finally, someone had the courage to contact the dean, at which point another professor was assigned to the class. In other words, if your professor is missing in action and does not respond, contact the appropriate person in the university. When we can't see each other in an office down the hall, real problems can go unnoticed!

Also, if you feel that your professor is not acting appropriately, it is your responsibility to speak up. Otherwise, you will not be the only victim. It can be especially difficult to address conflicts or harassment online. Look for the counselor, Ombuds, or other university office where you can get confidential advice about how to proceed.

Synchronous, asynchronous, or something inbetween?

As noted in Chapter 1, we can categorize the ways we communicate in terms of timing for the response to the initial message. As you can see in Figure 2.2, the same types of instructional or learning activities could be offered at the synchronous or asynchronous end of the continuum.

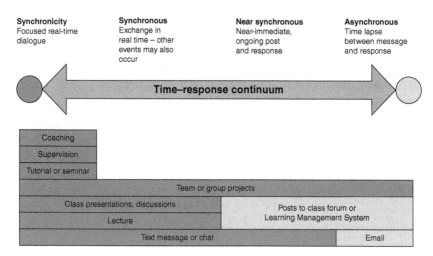

Figure 2.2   Time–response continuum and technologies

Learning with synchronicity (and what it means for you)

Synchronicity means we are not only online at the same time, we are all focused 100 per cent on the exchange. We have closed additional windows on our computers to eliminate distractions. This kind of interaction is essential when we are meeting one-to-one with the professor, tutor, teaching assistant, librarian, or other university personnel for coaching or supervision. We also want to focus closely when we are in a small group, such as a seminar or project check-in. We are expected to be engaged and to participate in these kinds of sessions.

Learning with synchronous communications (and what it means for you)

In a synchronous lecture, webinar, or online presentation, you are expected to be attentive, receptive, and respectful. Minimize distractions. Participation might be more limited than in meetings reliant on synchronicity, you need to take notes and prepare your questions. If you pose a question in this kind of event, try to articulate one where answers will be beneficial to others, rather than a specific question about your own work.

Synchronous can readily become near- or asynchronous when presentations are recorded and posted for viewing at your convenience. If so, you will need to use your own self-discipline to allocate time to view audiovisual materials with a minimum of distractions.

Learning with near synchronous communications (and what it means for you)

Discussion boards or forums are examples of near-synchronous communication. Everyone is not online at the same time, but the response expectations are within a specific time frame. Review expectations for the course about acceptable kinds of posts and timing for responses. You might be expected to submit academic writing with cited sources, or you might be expected to post more casual responses. See Chapters 4 and 5 for more about written assignments and peer exchange.

If you post as part of the class discussion, or ask a question, you will want others to reply on a timely basis. Show others the same courtesy! Be prompt and respectful with your comments.

Some online classes have more than one place for near synchronous communication. One area of the LMS board might be devoted to discussions about the readings and course content. Another area might be devoted to friendly, social interactions, a space for students to get acquainted and share informally. There might also be an area where you can post questions to the professor. If you have more personal or sensitive questions, contact your professor through email or make an appointment to consult one-to-one. Your professor will lay out the expectations for these different spaces, for example:

In addition to discussion assignments, the online class meeting space includes General Discussion areas: a CyberCafé and Ask Your Instructor. The Cyber-Café is an informal place for sharing, and Ask Your Instructor is a place to post general questions for me. If you have questions about your own work, contact me by email or we can arrange a phone conversation.

Learning with asynchronous communications (and what it means for you)

Email is typically used as an example of asynchronous communication. We all have expectations about response time; if you sent me an email would you expect me to respond today, tomorrow, or next week? In a fast-paced online class, you want to have a shared understanding of response time when you consult your professor. Given that online professors are exceptionally busy, do not wait until the last minute, or Friday evening, to ask a question.

Look for your professor's policies on email: do they want you to send emails or text messages with questions, or is there another preferred channel such as a private folder in the LMS?

Communication, learning and processing styles

Thinking processes mesh with online communications in e-learning. Think about your style(s) and preferences, and how you will use them. Look at the other styles and consider which you might need to adopt to succeed in online learning. For example, a confluent processor might need to work on social processing so they can succinctly communicate their big-picture views, or a social processor might need to focus on precise processing so they digest course details rather then expect others to explain everything.

- **Sequential processors**, as noted, might find the online course design is ready-made for their ways of thinking. With an established sequence of steps in place, they can look for ways to create meaningful learning experiences.

- **Precise processors** want all the details about the course content and assignments. This is a valuable trait in an online course where knowing exact expectations allows for planning and helps you avoid wasting precious time. Precise processors should avoid getting lost in the proverbial weeds. Highlight the top-level points such as major papers and due dates and absorb details as the weeks or learning units of the course progress.

- **Confluent processors** want to understand the course from a holistic perspective. They look at the course goals and objectives to gain this broad view. This is important and will be discussed in relation to assessment in Chapter 6. The confluent processor can see an expansive picture of the course that can seem overwhelming. While looking at the larger purpose of the course, they can forget to meet the week-by-week targets. Dividing bigger projects into smaller pieces and steps can suddenly make it seem doable. Confluent processors can create checklists and due date checkpoints to meet targets and achieve the big goal.

- **Technical processors** look for ways to construct something useful and apply course concepts. If application is not the focus of the course, they can use journaling or other techniques to make note of these practical ideas for future adoption. Technical processors can also focus on the ways in which concepts from the readings, experiences in discussions and learning activities allow them to build new knowledge throughout the term.

- **Social processors** look for opportunities to toss around ideas and hear others' perspectives. Depending on the nature of the course, they might be frustrated by the near synchronous, written forms of communication common to online learning. If so, social learners might want to look for study partners with similar propensities and set up regular times to converse.

You can also make use of the VAARWKO options for accessing materials and expressing yourself. Could you create a mind map or visual timeline for the course deliverables and due dates? Could you record your notes using your mobile device, instead of writing them? Listen to your own recordings to study or think about how to write on the topic? Set up audiovisual study sessions with friends to add social contact and avoid isolation?

ACTIVITY Developing your learning styles and processing traits

Look at your learning styles and processing characteristics:

I   How can you build on strengths and utilize your abilities as needed to achieve your goals and complete your online course(s)?

....

....

....

....

2   What new study, communication, or other skills will you need to develop?

....

....

....

....

3   Does your university offer any study skills workshops or resources to help you adapt to online learning?

....

....

....

....

Got it?

If I have been successful in face-to-face courses, can I adapt to an online course setting?

Got it!

If you are self-aware and know what works for you, you can use your innate skills and preferences while expanding your study skills and learning capacity. You will be able to understand and observe online course expectations and norms, without being constrained by them.

HOW DO I GET THE MOST FROM COURSE AND LIBRARY MATERIALS?

CHAPTER 3

60 second summary

To discover the best ways to use textbooks and electronic resources in an online course, begin with learning to use an online library or archive, and include making time to read and organize your textbooks and other materials. Use sources as evidence to support, or provide other perspectives about, the points you want to make. You will most likely use sources assigned for the course, and other sources you find and analyse. When academic institutions move to online learning, they often move to electronic course materials too. Learning to use a digital library is also part of this transition. Whether you are using paper or electronic resources, researching, evaluating, and organizing resources are positive skills and work habits. Continue in Chapter 4 to learn how to use critical reading and thinking skills to use these sources in assignments and papers.

INTRODUCTION

When you think about how to get the most out of the materials you read for the course, a related question undoubtedly surfaces: *how can I complete required readings in the most time-efficient way?* In this chapter, we will explore strategies that will help you do just that. The chapter includes suggestions for students at various academic levels, so use the advice that fits your own situation.

Keeping track of reading assignments is vital if you want to stay on top of your studies. Of course, you have to do research and reading whether you are studying online or not. While online course designs and instructional approach vary greatly, you will most likely have more independent reading in an online class. You will probably be asked to complete more digital library research activities and use electronic materials and media when studying online. Some kinds of academic work can be completed at the last minute, but reading is not one of them. This is especially true when you're working with scholarly articles, which involve being able to grasp complex theories and methods. Even experienced academics can't rush through research articles!

Understanding and organizing all research and reading assignments will help you draw value from this part of the learning experience, and successfully complete the course. It might seem tedious at first, but the time you put into creating a system that works for you will be time you save in the long run. You won't have to go through all the assignment assessment steps because you'll be able to look at assignments, and your calendar or diary, and know what time and steps will be needed to complete everything. You will be better prepared for more advanced studies, and the skills and techniques we will explore can be readily used in any class: online, face-to-face, or blended.

ASSESS THE REQUIREMENTS

Let's look at two broad types of readings: assigned or found. Assigned readings can include chapters in textbooks, articles, or case studies. You might also be expected to locate additional sources, evaluate, and read what you have found. Look closely at the syllabus and any other course materials and make note of what is expected of each type.

Assigned

Scan the syllabus and highlight all assigned readings. Make note of the number of pages, and timing for completion. Think about how much time it will take you to read that number of pages. If you don't know your reading pace, test yourself: time the reading for a textbook chapter. Given what you learn from the test, estimate how many pages you will need to read each day.

For larger assignments that continue for more than one week, unit, or lesson, break the readings down into manageable bites so you are not pressed for time when the deadline is near. Completing this reading tracker below will help you to remember your due dates and stay in control of prioritizing your work. For example:

Table 3.1   Reading tracker: example

Week, unit, or lesson of the course	Text or source	Pages	Time to read	Reading schedule
1	*Intro to Ethics*	Chapter 2, 150–225 (75 pages)	2.5 to 3 hours	Monday
1	'Practical ethics' article	15 pages	50 minutes	Tuesday
2–4	*Essays on Leadership and Ethics*	250 pages	9 hours	Week 2: 3 hours Week 3: 3 hours Week 4: 3 hours

 ## Track reading assignments

Here is a blank reading tracker you can use. Change or add columns to make it work for you!

Table 3.2   Reading tracker

Week, unit, or lesson of the course	Text or source	Pages	Time to read	Reading schedule

Week, unit, or lesson of the course	Text or source	Pages	Time to read	Reading schedule

Research assignments

With assigned readings you have three steps to complete: read it, make notes about the relevant points, and incorporate what you've learned into your writing, course projects, or discussions. With research assignments you have four additional steps to complete before you can begin your reading. First, you need to establish criteria for the search. Second, you need to conduct the search and locate a preliminary set of resources. Third, you need to do a preliminary review of the resources and select the ones that most closely meet assignment criteria. Fourth, you need to evaluate the quality of the resource. Now you are ready to start reading! Given these additional steps, more time will be needed to carry out assignments that require library research. You will need to map out, plan, and schedule these steps.

ESTABLISH CRITERIA FOR THE SEARCH

On what basis will you include or exclude sources? You cannot read every article published since the beginning of time! Particularly when searching in a digital library, a search can generate thousands of results. How will you narrow down the search results to a reasonable number that are going to be relevant to the project? After thinking through the assignment requirements and the direction you plan to take with the paper, establish some parameters.

Let's use an example as a way to think about inclusion and exclusion criteria. In this example, we are writing a paper about how cultural issues influence ways people work in teams. Here are some criteria we could consider:

- **Timeframe** We decide we want to include virtual teams, so we set the parameters as 2005–2020.

- **Local or global** Do we want to study this topic in the context of a community, country, region, or the whole world? We decide we will include global sources at the initial search stage, and might consider narrowing the focus to a region (e.g. the Americas), once we have an initial set of resources.

- **Discipline** Some researchers want to focus within their own field of study and select databases and journals accordingly. Think through your topic, where it is relevant in the world, and where it is widely studied. We might decide to hone in on research in our own fields in order to get a sense of the research foundations, or venture out of our home discipline to include a wider view.

  In our hypothetical example, we decide that while this paper is for a class in the education department, we want to take an interdisciplinary perspective. We want to understand issues in the workplace, which could have implications for ways educators prepare students for professional life. We decide to include research from the fields of business and sociology. Even though teamwork is studied in other fields, such as business, we will exclude them.

- **Methodology** Some researchers want to narrow results to qualitative, or quantitative, or mixed methods studies. We decide we want a variety of research articles.

- **Publication type** In addition to choosing what type of literature, we could choose whether we are open to including visual evidence or media, as well as or instead of written resources. We decide to include research articles, because we want to read about studies conducted by the writers themselves. We are not interested in theory at this time. We will include visuals or data visualizations from those studies as relevant.

Now that we know we are looking for contemporary research articles, from global perspectives in the fields of business and sociology, using any research methods, we can move to the next step.

 ACTIVITY Plan your library or online research

Think of a potential research topic related to your course of study that you can use for the activities in this chapter. Complete Table 3.3, considering the following questions. Partial criteria has been added to get your started.

- What criteria could you set to refine the topic and yield relevant sources?

- What do you want to be sure to include?

- What do you want to exclude at this point?

Table 3.3 Research criteria

Criteria	Include	Exclude	Notes
Timeframe			
Local or global			
Discipline			

(Continued)

Table 3.3 (Continued)

Criteria	Include	Exclude	Notes
Methodology			
Publication type			
Written or visual			

SEARCHING FOR SOURCES

You already know how to *search* online. You know how to use Google and find the information you need. Doing scholarly *research*, however, involves more than just knowing how to *search*. In fact, some of the ways you typically search *might be counterproductive* when it comes to doing research in library catalogs, article databases and other scholarly tools. Let's look at each step.

What types of resources can you use?

The types of resources that will be considered acceptable depend on the nature of the course, assignment requirements, and the level of academic study. Sources could include the types outlined in Table 3.4.

Table 3.4 Sources for academic assignments, papers, or projects

Books: Scholarly, fiction, essays	Photographs and images	Dissertations and theses
Magazines and newspaper articles	Movies, videos, DVDs	Scholarly articles

Diaries and journals	Audio recordings	Conference proceedings
Memoirs and autobiographies	Editorials or opinion pieces	Blog posts (look for professional, expert & academic blogs)
Interviews and speeches	Public opinion polls	Social media posts
Letters	Comics or graphic novels	Artwork
Professional writings		Graphics or visualizations
White papers or reports produced by businesses or organizations	Documents produced by government agencies, including congressional hearings and census records	Comments on websites or online communities

As you can see, there are many kinds of publicly available or library resources! We can find them on the open web with a general search, or by looking in the archives of public libraries, professional societies, non-profit organizations or NGOs, records from governments and businesses. Some resources are private and would require membership or permission to use. If you encounter these, consider asking whether educational access is available.

In a Masters or doctoral programme you'll be expected to primarily reference peer reviewed scholarly literature, but other sources can be used to understand contemporary contexts for the issues being studied. In an undergraduate course a wide range of sources might be acceptable. In a more practical or applied programme of study, popular or professional resources might be acceptable. If the assignment expectations are unclear, ask before you start doing your research.

Let's look at our hypothetical topic again: how cultural issues influence ways people work in teams. If we can include contemporary sources, we could look for:

- Professional writings by people who work in global business settings, from business-oriented magazines or white papers
- Professional writings by sociologists and social observers
- Business association blogs, newsletters, or conference proceedings
- Social media hashtags and online discussion groups about global teams
- Cultural background information from sources in the countries that interest us.

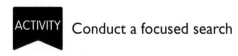 Conduct a focused search

Using the research topic you have identified for these activities find at least three sources that feature current thinking related to your assignment or paper.

Source 1: ....

Source 2: ....

Source 3: ....

Why would you use these sources in an assignment?

....

Why would you reject these sources for an assignment?

....

Peer-reviewed literature

The terms *scholarly journal* or *academic journal* signal to you that it is a peer-reviewed publication. Peer review is considered the most rigorous and respected form of editorial review. It is a multistage process for determining whether articles, papers, chapters, or books get published, require revisions, or are rejected. Getting published in these journals is highly competitive.

Scholarly or academic journal articles are universally subjected to this kind of scrutiny to evaluate the credibility of the research and clarity of the writing. To ensure greater independence and objectivity in the peer reviewing process, blind reviews are used, which means reviewers do not know the identities of the authors and the other reviewers and the authors do not know the identities of the reviewers. Reviewers are experts in the field of study.

Types of scholarly articles

There are three main kinds of scholarly journal articles. You might decide you want to focus on one type in your search or look for a variety of articles.

1   **Research** These articles are reports on original empirical research. They are typically formatted with four main sections:

   - *Introduction*, with the purpose of the study, and context within the literature

   - *Methods*, with a description of the qualitative or quantitative procedures used to conduct the investigation

   - *Results,* which explain what the researcher found

   - *Discussion,* which includes a summary of the study and implications for other research or for practice.

2   **Literature reviews** Literature reviews are articles that present an analysis of other scholars' research. In this category you might also find *meta-analyses* – articles describing the large-scale statistical analysis of data collected by multiple researchers, or metasynthesis – articles describing the qualitative analysis of data collected by multiple researchers.

3   **Theoretical** Articles that discuss perspectives on theories, describe tests of theoretical constructs, or present new thinking about theories.

Primary or secondary sources?

Another way to differentiate your sources is by finding out whether they are primary or secondary sources. One way to define *primary* sources is that they were written by the original thinker or researcher. If you conduct and publish a study about student success, you would be the *primary source* for the findings you put forward. If another researcher discussed your study, their work would be a *secondary source* about student success. Looking at the types of literature above, research articles, and theoretical articles, these are generally the primary work of the writers. Literature reviews are generally secondary sources since they discuss other researchers' work.

Primary sources can be looked at another way, as those created during the time period being studied, reflecting the individual viewpoints of participants or observers to that event. By this definition, a secondary source is a work that interprets or analyses an historical event or phenomenon. It is generally at least one step removed from the event and is often based on primary sources. Whenever you want to get to the beginning of a school of thought or kind of experience, look for primary sources. When you want to know about the explanations and updated ideas, look for secondary sources.

Open access or subscription?

As a student you most likely have access to a digital academic library. The library subscribes to various publications and to databases that include numerous journals, case studies, eBooks, and media. However, if you find a source not available through your library, you will see that individual subscriptions are very pricey, indeed the purchase price of a single article could cover your coffee budget for the week. In such situations you can look for open access journal articles. An increasing number of scholarly journals are freely available online; you can find a global collection at the Directory of Open Access Journals, or www.doaj.org.

Researchers often share pre-publication copies of their articles on their own websites, on their university websites, or on online academic communities such as ResearchGate. If you really hit a brick wall and are unable to access an article that interests you, write to the author and ask for a copy.

CONDUCT THE DIGITAL LIBRARY SEARCH

It is time to visit your library and search for books and articles. You might be surprised to find that there is not one search engine that works for the entire library collection. Instead, you will probably see a list of databases. Each one contains a proprietary set of archives. Some are broadly multidisciplinary, and others are narrowly focused. Your library subscribes to the databases that relate to subjects commonly studied in your institution. Within the databases are additional subscription choices, so you might find you are blocked from reading articles because that journal is not one your institution chose to offer.

SAGE Publications' databases include:

- SAGE journals: Access articles in journals published by SAGE.

- SAGE Knowledge: Access reference books and media published by SAGE and Corwin press, covering the social sciences, business, and education.

- SAGE Research Methods: Access books, articles, media and case studies, as well as instructional materials about research methods.

Other databases your library might carry

- EBSCO: includes numerous databases, including Academic Search, a multi-disciplinary social sciences collection, Business Source, Sociology Source, Humanities Source, and others

- ERIC: Education Resources Information Center, education-related literature

- PsycINFO: Psychology journals

- JSTOR: Multidisciplinary sources

- ScienceDirect and Scopus: Academic books and articles published by Elsevier

- Web of Science: Journals on arts and humanities, social and natural sciences.

Choosing keywords

When you open a database, you will have search options based on key words. To select keywords:

- Identify the main concepts of your topic

- Use a thesaurus or brainstorm synonyms and antonyms

- Find out what terms were previously used to describe new or emerging topics.

Most databases allow either a basic or advanced search. The basic search involves just entering one or more keywords and clicking 'search' or the search icon. You could use the basic search option, such as the one for SAGE journals shown in Figure 3.1, to get an initial sense of whether your keywords are too general (you find zillions of sources) or too specific (you find ten sources). Either is a signal that you need to reframe your keywords.

Figure 3.1   Basic search on SAGE journals

In an advanced search you can also specify whether you want articles with the keyword anywhere in the article, in the title, abstract, or author-provided keywords. You can enter the criteria you identified and indicate the timeframe and other parameters. Some advanced searches allow you to use the criteria you selected in relation to discipline.

If you want to search within a specific journal, enter the name, or leave it blank to search all books, journals, media, in that database.

In the advanced search you can limit results to sources you have access to, in other words, the journals your library has chosen for full subscriptions. You can also choose open access, which would be freely available outside the library.

Using other search features

Once you know the journals that fit your research, you can also browse within the journal. SAGE journal homepages highlight new or popular articles.

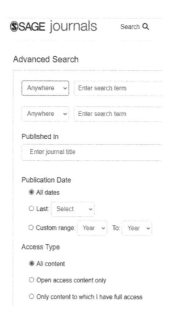

Figure 3.2   SAGE Journals advanced search: step 1

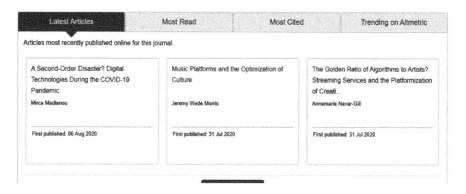

Figure 3.3   SAGE Journals advanced search: step 2

You can browse by year or issue or look for special-focus issues.

Once you have located articles, you can use them to find other sources by looking for related articles, similar articles, or keywords. You can also mine the reference list for sources.

Defining search terms

Continuing with our example, now we need to define the search terms and keywords we will enter into the databases we selected.

Figure 3.4   SAGE Journals advanced search: step 3

The topic has two concepts: *cultural issues* and *teamwork*. We can think about synonyms for these terms that could provide more results but might also take the search into new directions. For example, synonyms for *culture* include *arts*, and *ethnicity*. Synonyms for *teamwork* include *collaboration* and *solidarity*. But are we interested in *artistic collaboration*? Are we interested in *solidarity* and *ethnicity*? Being specific will be important.

Entering "culture and team*" into the general search box for the SAGE journals database yielded 149451 results. With the same "culture and team*" keywords in the advanced search by title and limited to 2005–2020, results were narrowed down to 74, with 61 research articles. After reviewing the result list, I can exclude some that are about sports teams. If I need more sources, I can:

- Try entering keywords with different search parameters, from specific to general, such as:

  1 Keyword as title

  2 Keyword in abstract

  3 Keyword in 'author's keywords'

  4 Keyword in full-text

- Change the keywords.
- Look in other databases.

 ACTIVITY Find and explore databases

I Given the topic you have identified for these activities, select a database in your library.

2 Identify keywords and search using both basic and advanced methods.

3 Try the same search in a different database.

4 Choose the most relevant three sources that feature current thinking related to your assignment or paper.

ORGANIZE SOURCES

The sources you locate for one course might be of value as you continue your studies. Develop a system for keeping track of the articles and sources you have found. Think about how to organize sources on your computer for easy retrieval later. Create folders by topic or course number. Some save articles by author name, others by title. You could use a table such as Table 3.5 to save notes, or a reference manager software tool. (For more on using these kinds of tools, see Chapter 4.)

Table 3.5 Literature table

Citation	Methodology	Theory/ Conceptual framework	Population/ Sample	Data collection methods	Data analysis methods	Notes

Literature table (add columns for other types of information important to your study)

Literature table (add columns for other types of information important to your study)

Citation	Methodology	Theory/ Conceptual framework	Population/ Sample	Data collection methods	Data analysis methods	Notes

 **Categorize sources**

Create a table or another system and categorize the three sources you found that relate to your topic.

A student told us

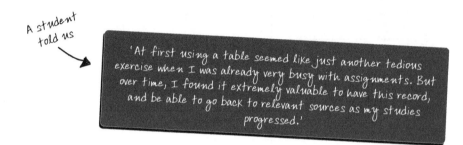

'At first using a table seemed like just another tedious exercise when I was already very busy with assignments. But over time, I found it extremely valuable to have this record, and be able to go back to relevant sources as my studies progressed.'

EVALUATE SOURCES

An important step when finding your resources is to make sure they are of high quality – otherwise, any conclusions you draw from your reading and research may not be as accurate.

Use this checklist when evaluating the quality of resources.

Authority

Who is the author? Is the author credible?

What else has the author written?

Is the author transparent about any biases?

In which communities and contexts does the author have expertise?

o   Does the author represent a particular set of world views?

o   Do they represent specific gender, sexual, racial, political, social, and/or cultural orientations?

o   Do they privilege some sources of authority over others?

Scholarship and purpose

Is the purpose clear?

Who is the intended audience?

o   Is it for scholars or students?

o   Is it for practising professionals?

o   Is it for a general audience?

If it is a research article, what is the research approach?

o   Questions?

o   Methodology?

o   Theoretical framework?

o   Sample?

o   Context?

Publication and format

Is the resource accurate and free of errors?

Was it published in a scholarly or reputable publication, such as an academic journal or edited collection?

o   Who was the publisher? Was it a university press or recognized publisher? Commercial publisher?

o   Was it self-published?

o   Was it formally peer-reviewed? If not, were there outside editors or reviewers?

Does the publication have a particular editorial position?

o   Is it generally thought to be a conservative or progressive outlet?

o   Is the publication sponsored by any other companies or organizations? Do the sponsors have particular biases?

Relevance

Does the resource present a balanced argument?

How is it relevant to your research?

o   Is it a primary source?

o   If secondary, does it discuss the primary sources that you are studying?

What is the scope of coverage?

o   Is it global or local, a general overview or an in-depth analysis?

o   Does the scope match your assignment needs?

o   Is the time period and geographic region relevant to your research?

What is the history of scholarship on the topic?

o   How did one researcher build on earlier theories and research?

o   Does new research agree or disagree with earlier assumptions and findings?

o   Does the researcher point to seminal work you need to find and read?

Date of publication

When was the source first published?

Is the resource up to date?

What version or edition of the source are you consulting?

Are there any published reviews, responses, or rebuttals?

Documentation

Did they cite their sources?

o   If not, do you have any other means to verify the reliability of their claims?

Look closely at the quotations and paraphrases from other sources:

o   Did they appropriately represent the context of their cited sources?

o   Did they ignore any important elements from their cited sources?

   o   Are they cherry-picking facts to support their own arguments?

   o   Did they appropriately cite ideas that were not their own?

Has the resource been cited by other researchers?

 Evaluate sources

Use two of the sources you located, either two academic articles or an article and a piece you found online. Work through the checklist and compare and contrast the two resources.

e-TEXTBOOKS

How do you prefer to study with textbooks? Are you accustomed to print books that allow you to write in the margins, and highlight text you want to revisit later? Do you use sticky notes on pages for future reference?

Figure 3.5   A well-used print textbook!

Or do you prefer electronic textbooks that allow you to carry a large pile of otherwise heavy books on a laptop or tablet? Electronic and print books have equivalent content, but of course they function differently. As shown in Figure 3.6 in electronic texts, you can highlight key points, make notes, or save text to reference in a paper.

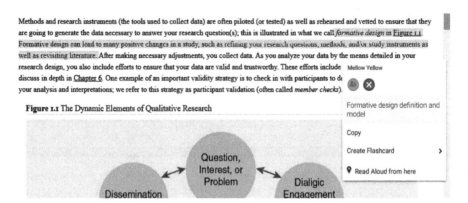

Figure 3.6   Electronic highlighting

Sometimes you have a choice and can select the type you like best, in other situations the institution has made a choice and all students must follow it. The textbooks might be included in tuition or course fees or integrated into the Learning Management System.

If you have a choice, what will be most important, given your own learning style and approach to reading? What your friend sees as an advantage, you might see as a disadvantage. Use Table 3.6 to make some notes about the features you want in a textbook, then continue to the next section where you can plan to make the best use of the text, in whatever form it is available.

Table 3.6 Print or electronic resources?

Print books	Electronic books	Notes: my learning styles and preferences
You can save the book for future reference	You might only have access for the term when you are using the book in a course	
You can loan the book to a friend. You can sell the book at the end of the term	You cannot transfer ownership	
New editions mean buying another book	Automatic updates	
Log into a book website to access additional resources	e-textbooks include embedded audio and video, and external links for additional information or learning activities	
Print books can be read anywhere, even if you do not have an internet connection	While some platforms allow for offline reading, interactive e-textbook features require a computer/tablet and high-speed internet	
Highlight and write with pens and pencils	Highlight electronically. Highlights or notes are saved in a notebook you can print, share with study partners, or save to use in other applications	
No accessibility features	Ability to change font size and spacing. Read-aloud text-to-speech	
Print textbooks allow for more focus, without temptation to visit social media	e-textbooks are read on computers or devices, with other distractions a tap away	
You use the table of contents or index to search	You can search within the book using keywords	

Electronic books, analogue notes

If you are someone who resists electronic texts, you can still use an analogue approach to take notes. In your paper journal, indicate the page number or location of the text when you record your notes. You might want to create sections in your journal for each chapter, so your notes align with the text and you can easily find the points you recorded. You could create additional sections of the journal for reflections and observations, or project plans.

Analogue books, digital notes

If you would prefer an eText, but it is not available, consider using an electronic notebook to keep your notes about a print text. Select a notetaking software product that allows you to access notes across devices. That way you can see notes you took on your mobile phone when you are studying on your laptop.

PLAN AND TRACK READING-RELATED ASSIGNMENTS

Create a table or spreadsheet that works for you, depending on how many assignments and deliverables you need to complete. Keep it simple and usable. Enter all the target and firm dates for process steps and due dates into your calendar or diary so you can plan other personal, professional, or academic activities around them. For example, see Table 3.7.

What are you supposed to *do* with the readings? Go to Chapter 5 for the next steps!

 ACTIVITY Make your own reading tracker

Use Table 3.8 or create another system for tracking assigned and research reading requirements and adapt column headings to your own coursework.

Table 3.7 Reading assignment tracker: Example

Module or week of the course	Assignment title	Notes and/or questions	Requirements • Length • Number of sources	Research & reading plan	Date for completing step or draft	Final due date
1	Review assignment for annotated bibliography required as a step in the process of completing the research paper.	Topic: ethics and team leaders Question: can I include articles about public sector leaders or only studies about business leaders?	20 sources	Put assignment into course schedule and plan each step		Friday of week 6
1	Annotated bibliography, step 1 Criteria from assignment: peer reviewed sources no more than 5 years past publication date.	Step 1: Identify search terms and keywords		Step 1: Identify search terms and keywords	Friday of week 1	
2		Step 2: Conduct literature search			Friday of week 2	
3		Step 3: Organize and review sources			Friday of week 3	
4		Step 4: Evaluate sources			Friday of week 4	
5		Read selected articles and make notes			Friday of week 5	
6		Complete annotations and submit			Friday of week 6	
7–8	Work on draft of the paper for preliminary review		Discuss 20 sources in the draft		Friday of week 10	

Table 3.8 Reading tracker table

Module or week of the course	Assignment title	Notes and/or questions	Requirements • Length • Number of sources	Research & reading plan	Date for completing step or draft	Final due date

Adapt techniques to fit your study style

Look at your earlier activities. Answer the following questions:

How can you adapt these techniques to fit your courses and personal study style?

....

....

....

....

How can you adopt this kind of systematic planning into your regular study mode?

....

....

....

....

Got it?

Can I find credible resources online without being overwhelmed by lots of irrelevant junk?

Got it.

By understanding what makes a resource credible, developing specific search criteria, and by using my academic library and other reputable sites, I can find the resources I need.

HOW DO I CREATE MY BEST WRITTEN WORK?

CHAPTER 4

60 second summary

The assignments for an online learning course may be identical to those you have completed previously, but the process may be different. In a face-to-face class the professor might take time to explain expectations and requirements, and answer questions. In an online class, professors assume that you can grasp this information from the syllabus or posted assignment instructions. In other words, in online learning you need to take more responsibility for reviewing course materials, and asking questions in a timely fashion when clarification is needed. You also need to take more responsibility for organizing your time and work. The suggestions in this chapter will help you to do just that.

INTRODUCTION

Excellent written work is the focus for Chapter 4. In Chapter 5 we will think about how to create excellent work together, in projects and interactions with peers. In Chapter 6 we will look at feedback and assessments.

Much of what you will explore in this chapter applies in any academic context; it is not unique to online learning. It is applicable to online learning though, because when studying online you will most likely have more learning in the form of reading and writing. Also, you might be completing work more independently. The impetus is on you to develop your own systems for managing your time and work.

For the purpose of this chapter, we will use the term 'assignment' to refer to any course requirement that you will submit. It could be a research paper, a project, or an exercise. It could be a single deliverable, or a complex series of drafts that are reviewed and revised for a final submission. If you are studying for a Masters or doctoral degree, you will have an overarching goal: to complete a thesis or dissertation. If that is your situation, you are looking beyond individual assignments. You are thinking, collecting resources, and developing preliminary work you will build on over the timeframe of your programme. Adapt and apply suggestions offered here to your own needs and preferences and the requirements of the course or programme.

FIRST, UNDERSTAND THE ASSIGNMENT

How can you meet expectations unless you know what is expected?

In Chapter 3 you thought through how to develop search criteria to use when looking for resources to use in your academic writing, and you looked at how to evaluate those sources so you can discern credibility and quality. Next, you need to decide what to do with those sources. Figuring this out *before* you dig into reading will save time and frustration.

In a face-to-face class, the professor, tutor, instructor or lecturer can easily explain course requirements and expectations for papers, projects, and/or assignments. While (as discussed in Chapter 2) your professor is there, on the other side of the screen, in online learning you must rely more on documents such as the syllabus and written descriptions of the work to be completed. These documents will not only tell you what is due when, they will also help you understand the criteria that will be used to determine your grade. (See Chapter 6 for guidance on feedback and assessments.) If, after reading course documents and this chapter, you do not understand the assignment(s), ask for clarification before moving ahead. This point cannot be emphasized strongly enough: do not wait to ask questions if you do not understand the assignment. Delays only waste your time and your professor's time.

Bloom's Taxonomy will help you decode expectations

When you look critically at course and assignment materials, you will start to see the same action words used to describe the precise types of learning expected. Words such as 'evaluate', 'analyse' and 'interpret' can be used for a whole course, and for specific assignments. Many educational institutions use a system known as *Bloom's Taxonomy* to articulate learning goals and objectives. It was developed in the 1950s and updated in 2000 (Anderson et al., 2000; Bloom et al., 1956). We will use the updated version.

When you understand this taxonomy you can use it to understand an assignment more precisely, so you will not waste time on extraneous or irrelevant steps.

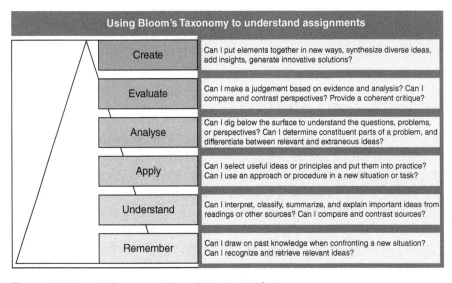

Using Bloom's Taxonomy to understand assignments

Create	Can I put elements together in new ways, synthesize diverse ideas, add insights, generate innovative solutions?
Evaluate	Can I make a judgement based on evidence and analysis? Can I compare and contrast perspectives? Provide a coherent critique?
Analyse	Can I dig below the surface to understand the questions, problems, or perspectives? Can I determine constituent parts of a problem, and differentiate between relevant and extraneous ideas?
Apply	Can I select useful ideas or principles and put them into practice? Can I use an approach or procedure in a new situation or task?
Understand	Can I interpret, classify, summarize, and explain important ideas from readings or other sources? Can I compare and contrast sources?
Remember	Can I draw on past knowledge when confronting a new situation? Can I recognize and retrieve relevant ideas?

Figure 4.1 Bloom's Taxonomy with assignment questions

How can this model help you decide what is needed from resources that were assigned or found in your research? Here is an example. Let's say you are studying empowerment in the workplace using Albert Bandura's (1997) self-efficacy theory.

For an assignment that asks you to:

- **Remember**. You will define the basic concepts of self-efficacy theory and be prepared to recall them in this and other assignments or tests. Additional verbs associated with the *remember* level: choose, define, list, name, tell, select.

- **Understand**. You will be able to summarize and classify the four main constructs and explain them in the context of the articles and/or textbook readings. Additional verbs associated with the *understand* level: explain, outline, show, demonstrate.

- **Apply**. You will be able to use the four constructs of self-efficacy theory to suggest new policies for training managers. Additional verbs associated with the *apply* level: model, organize, plan, construct, build.

- **Analyse**. You will be able to grasp why Bandura developed this theory, the research foundations, and the ways the theory has been used for research and practice in fields such as business, education, and psychology. Additional verbs associated with the *analyse* level: dissect, distinguish, examine, infer.

- **Evaluate**. You will be able to compare and contrast self-efficacy theory with empowerment theory (Zimmerman, 2000). Additional verbs associated with the *evaluate* level: criticize, judge, measure, recommend, estimate.

- **Create**. You will be able to add new constructs to self-efficacy theory that take into account more recent research about success factors of remote workers. Additional verbs associated with the *create* level: adapt, design, develop, formulate, originate.

Of course, the same assignment could include learning activities at multiple levels. I might need to show I *understand* theories before I *analyse* them. But if I assumed that describing how I *understand* the theory will fulfil the paper's requirements, while the professor expected I would *analyse* the theory, we would have a disconnect (and I would have to take the time necessary to do more reading and revise the paper). By clarifying one or more types of learning activities, I will be prepared to start reading critically.

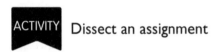

ACTIVITY Dissect an assignment

Look at a research paper assignment for a current or recent course. Read the assignment description and find the verbs or other words that denote actions to be taken. To what level of Bloom's Taxonomy do they correspond? Knowing what you know now, how would you position your work to align with expectations laid out in the assignment?

Action verb 1:	Bloom's Taxonomy level:
Action verb 2:	Bloom's Taxonomy level:
Action verb 3:	Bloom's Taxonomy level:

To excel in this assignment, I should:

....

....

....

....

READ CRITICALLY

Bloom showed that being able to *evaluate* is a higher-order critical-thinking skill. You will be using these skills when you read academic articles. In Chapter 3 you looked at ways to evaluate a source and decide whether or not it fits with your assignment, paper, or project. Now, evaluate what you can use and learn from these sources by reading critically and taking notes that will allow you to access and build on the ideas presented in the book, article, or media piece.

The most fundamental expectation of academic writing is that the claims you make will be backed up with reasons based on some form of evidence. 'So the reader asks at every point: "Have you given me sufficient grounds for accepting your claim?"' (Wallace and Wray, 2016, p. 20). This means you are not only reading carefully to get all the major points; you are also reading to look beneath the author's points.

When you review the paper or project requirements through the Bloom's Taxonomy lens, you can identify key questions you will try to answer when you are reading. For example:

- **Reading to *Remember* and *Understand*.** Look for definitions of key terms, main ideas, and concepts. Is the problem or issue clearly and accurately defined?

- **Reading to *Apply*.** Look for specific examples of how others have used the ideas, or ways the writers explained how to use the ideas. Do the writers explain why these ideas or approaches fit the problem?

- **Assignment that asks you to *Analyse*.** Look for writings that differentiate the source from others, or that structure, or organize ideas. Is the writer expressing an opinion or biased perspective? Are they transparent about it?

- **Assignment that asks you to *Evaluate*.** Look for tests or critiques of the ideas. Is the claim, argument, or research credible?

- **Assignment that asks you to *Create*.** Look for source material you can draw on to design or construct a new idea or new way of thinking about the problem. Do the writers offer the basis for building on their work?

Reading research articles

Let's apply these ideas to research articles. When classes shift online, professors make more use of digital resources. That can mean more research articles and fewer print textbooks. If you are an experienced student you have undoubtedly discovered ways to read journal articles, but these tips might help if you are a new student.

For this example, we will use this open access article:

Litt, E., Zhao, S., Kraut, R. and Burke, M. (2020). What Are Meaningful Social Interactions in Today's Media Landscape? A Cross-Cultural Survey. Social Media + Society. https://doi.org/10.1177/2056305120942888

The article follows the typical journal format.

- **Introduction**. This section helps you *understand* the problem the researchers studied, with references to literature that supports their perspectives. They spelled out their purpose: "The goal of this research is to examine meaningful social interactions in today's media landscape, and what makes some interactions more meaningful than others" (Litt et al., 2020, p. 2). Pay attention to introductions if you want to learn how to define research problems.

- **Literature review**. In this section the researchers *analyse* and *evaluate* the literature that supports their study. In this article, they organize the literature into three main topic areas. Pay attention to literature reviews to familiarize yourself with literature on the defined problem, and to learn skills you can *apply* when you need to craft a literature review for a paper, thesis, or dissertation.

- **Methods**. In this section the researchers *create* a design for the study, supported by their evaluations and analyses of the problem and preceding studies. Pay attention to methods to learn about research design and methods to conduct studies.

- **Discussion**. In this section the researchers *analyse* their findings. In this particular article they begin to *create* a 'Framework for Social Interactions' (Litt et al., 2020). Pay attention to the discussion sections of articles to understand the findings and their implications.

- **Limitations**. In this section the researchers *evaluate* the parameters of the study. Pay attention to the discussion sections of articles to understand gaps in the research and opportunities for your own potential studies to build on the inquiry described in the article.

- **Conclusions**. In the final section of the article, the researcher ties the pieces together and evaluates the literature, empirical methods, findings, and implications.

When you understand how research articles are structured, you can be strategic about your reading. For example, if I am interested in survey design, I might read the whole article through, then do deep reading and notetaking in the Methods section. If I am interested in social media interactions, I might do deep reading and notetaking in the Introduction and Discussion sections.

 Critical reading with questions in mind

These are some critical reading questions for a research article. How would you categorize them? What would you add?

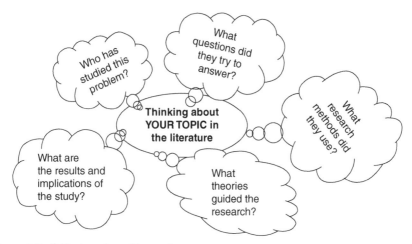

Figure 4.2 Critical reading with questions

Given your own field of study and the subject matter for your courses, what questions should you ask when you read?

1 ....

2 ....

3 ....

Categorize methods and findings as you read research articles

When you are doing a lot of academic reading it can all become a blur. Which article was it that describes this problem so clearly? Which methodologist explained how to conduct interviews? You can waste a lot of time trying to locate that great example you read an hour ago. It is even more challenging when you need to find the article you know fits perfectly, but you read it last term. Where is it now?

It is to your advantage to develop a system of highlighting and note-taking that becomes habitual. Once you have completed your reading, organize your sources using topic-specific folders on your computer (explained in Chapter 3) and/or a reference manager (explained in the next section of this chapter.) Your system will not be productive unless you use it consistently. Again, it has to be your approach, one that fits your own reading and learning styles. Adapt the ideas suggested here to work for you!

In Chapter 3 you learned how to establish criteria for efficient searches in a digital library. Use those criteria – and/or others that fit your assignment or project – as the basis for your system. If you are highlighting sources, keep the same colour scheme for every document. If you need more colours than Word allows with the highlight feature, change text colours. Now, if you are looking through your articles for one that used qualitative methods, you know you are looking for pink, versus quantitative, always blue. You might highlight Learning theory in yellow, and Pedagogy in green.

 Identify keywords for your assignment or research topic

List the important key words for:

a)   the current assignment

....

b) your ongoing work.

....

Create your own coding system. Save it to your desktop or print it out and keep it close to your workspace so you can remember it.

Make notes on what you read

Be sure your critical reading system includes a way to keep notes. Once again, create a system that is comfortable for you, and use it consistently! In his blog called 'Note-taking expert', Dr Nick Blackbourn observes that notes are a worthwhile exercise for three reasons:

*   To recall information

*   To understand information

*   To make connections between ideas.

These are the fundamental aspects of acquiring knowledge and, subsequently, being able to apply this knowledge to creatively solve problems. It is the cognitive effort of making notes – actively grappling with new ideas – that provides the means to reflect, process, and internalize new concepts (Blackbourn, 2020).

Blackbourn (2020) suggests that the basic character of notes can be boiled down to three components:

*   **Summarize**. Rewrite concepts in your own words. Don't simply copy them verbatim. Rather, synthesize what you've learned in a way that reflects your unique approach.

*   **Critique**. What is particularly noteworthy? Is there anything you agree with or disagree with? Ask questions of the material and try not to take it at face value.

- **Follow-up questions**. What would you like further information on? Either for general interest, or to validate or disprove an aspect of what you're reading.

The first type, summarize, is probably the most familiar. We record main points in a succinct way. The next level, critique, allows us to dig into the evidence. Finally, by making notes about questions, you can identify new angles to research and build upon. Ideally, the first take would be to summarize, then to critique and identify questions.

You have a number of process options:

- Do you want to take notes on one reading at a time, or organize note by topic, across multiple sources? In other words, have one document with all your notes about ten articles you read that mentioned 'leadership', or ten documents for ten articles?
- Do you want to use a table, such as those shown in Chapter 3?
- Do you want to create an outline for the paper, and add notes and citations into the section where you will include them?
- Do you make notes in sequence as you read, then think about how you will cite relevant points in the assignment?

Given the online context, what digital tools do you prefer:

- Do you want to make notes on the article file or eBook, or in a separate document?
- Do you want to use a note-taking application that can be read across devices, such as Evernote or OneNote?
  - o OneNote is part of Microsoft Office, so you might already have it. It is an electronic loose-leaf binder that allows you to organize notes into sections, add pages, type anywhere, include images, screen captures, tables, audio and video notes. You can use your keywords to tag content. OneNote can be accessed on multiple devices – phones, computers,

tablets, iOS or Android. Content created in OneNote integrates with other Microsoft products and can be printed and shared collaboratively with others using OneDrive.

o   Evernote is an application that works similarly. It has free and premium versions. You might have another application on your computer; the brand is not important, find the one with features you like and use it consistently.

- Do you want to use a tablet and digital pen, so your handwritten notes are saved electronically?

- Do you want to write notes by hand on paper, while you read books and articles on a screen?

- Do you prefer to write notes, or speak them? You could use voice-to-text for note taking, speaking your notes while reading.

Here are some additional note-taking tips.

- Make sure your notes capture all the information you need – including bibliographical data, publisher details, page numbers and quotes. (See information below about reference manager software.)

- Make sure your notes are legible, succinct, and relevant.

ACTIVITY Improve your note-taking skills

Download two different kinds of academic articles, one research article and one that is a literature review. In addition, download a video, podcast, webinar recording, or other media related to your assignment or research. Use these sources as the basis for a note-taking exercise. Try a couple of tools and techniques introduced in this chapter and decide which you want to use with your next readings or for taking notes about other kinds of media.

Article 1: ....

Notes

Article 2: ....

Notes

Media piece: ....

Notes

PREPARE TO CREATE EXCELLENT WRITTEN ASSIGNMENTS

Much online learning is completed in writing. This is particularly true in online classes that take place in Learning Management Systems or in situations where asynchronous communications aim to include geographically dispersed students (see Chapter 1). Honing your skills in grammar, spelling, and organization will be very beneficial, whether you are writing comments in an online discussion or drafting a major research paper. Keep in mind that you will create an impression for your online instructor with your writing. Sloppy, incomplete writing, submitted at the last minute, will not create a good impression and show you as a serious student.

Written discussions

Whereas a face-to-face class might include formal and informal conversation, online class discussion often takes place using asynchronous forum posts and comments. This means your professor will post questions, and students will post answers. Students are typically expected to comment to their peers. Look for the expectations. We will look at ways to collaborate in online discussions in Chapter 5.

Literature-based written assignments

Sometimes you will be asked to dig deeply into each source, and other times you will be asked to analyse a group of articles.

- **Annotated bibliography**. An annotated bibliography is YOUR analysis of each article, with YOUR discussion of it as each source relates to your paper. What are the key points of each article – the problem studied, perspective taken, the research and its findings?

- **Literature review**. A literature review is an account of what has been published on a topic by accredited scholars and researchers. It is a focused exploration of the research that has been conducted about a selected issue, topic or question.

In contrast to the deep dive into each particular article for the annotated bibliography, for a literature review you will analyse, compare and contrast a group of sources.

Once you have collected book chapters, articles, and other materials you need for a paper or project, you need to look critically across the entire set to answer questions such as:

o   What are the relationships across the selection of articles?

o   How do the definitions, explanations and approaches compare and contrast?

o   How do theories/methodologies/methods compare and contrast?

o   What are the themes and trends in this body of work?

Write your assignment

Now that you have analysed the expectations for the assignment, plan for the process and timing to complete it. If your professor offers to review an outline or draft, take advantage of the opportunity and build that step into your plan. Being able to get feedback is important.

Academic writing asks you to go a step farther than you do in everyday writing. You need to develop your own voice. In other words, while you need to ground your writing in evidence from the literature and reliable sources, you also need to present your points in your own unique way. Looking at Bloom again, academic writing uses all levels, and when you *create* new insights you develop your scholarly voice. This takes time, practice, and courage.

Your writing plan should include a systematic structure with a logical argument and you should follow it step-by-step. Make sure you answer the question clearly and succinctly, including plenty of evidence to support your theories, and that the citations and references are correctly presented, in line with your assignment guidelines. (See more about references in the next section.)

Here are three recommendations for essays and research papers:

1 **Write clearly.** You don't have to use big words to sound academic, but you do have to understand the words you are using and spell them correctly.

2 **Present an objective, well-balanced argument.** Support both sides of your arguments with credible evidence.

3 **Keep to a logically organized structure.** Take your reader on a well-signposted journey and don't throw in any surprises. Use headings and subheadings to structure long papers. Most assignments are made up of three sections: an *introduction*, a *main part*, and a summary *conclusion*.

- Your *introduction* should include a brief explanation of what will be discovered in your work, where, when and why.

- The *main section* is where you show the supporting and opposing evidence for your argument. Signpost your reader with a gradual and logical progression through and throughout your work. Each paragraph should have one main idea that is supported with evidence and analysis. Aim for one point per sentence, 3–5 sentences per paragraph and three paragraphs per page. Provide transitions to link one paragraph to the next. Present the paper using the style and format laid out in the syllabus or assignment instructions.

- In the *conclusion*, summarize your main points or answers without introducing any new information.

 Review your own writing

Pull out a recent written assignment or essay.

Critique the structure:

....

....

....

....

(Continued)

How could you have organized it differently?

....

....

....

....

REFERENCE ALL SOURCES

It is critical that you list all sources, including media, websites, and online resources. If you use someone else's ideas, you must respect them by crediting their work with a citation. Academic institutions typically adopt a system of references that spells out the format to use. Three of the most common ones are the American Psychological Association (APA), Modern Language Association (MLA), and Chicago. Each of these has a publication manual that is updated every few years. They provide guidance on formatting of papers as well as citations and reference lists.

While they all include the same basic components, the format of a citation varies with each of these systems. Also, the format varies for each type of source. For example, here are some variations in APA Style:

Article:

Jerrentrup, A., Mueller, T., Glowalla, U., Herder, M., Henrichs, N., Neubauer, A. and Schaefer, J. R. (2018). Teaching medicine with the help of 'Dr. House.' *PLoS ONE, 13*(3), Article e0193972. https://doi.org/10.1371/journal.pone.0193972

Book:

Sapolsky, R. M. (2017). *Behave: The biology of humans at our best and worst.* Penguin Books.

Chapter in edited book:

Dillard, J. P. (2020). Currents in the study of persuasion. In M. B. Oliver, A. A. Raney, and J. Bryant (Eds.), *Media effects: Advances in theory and research* (4th ed., pp. 115–129). Routledge.

Facebook post:

News From Science. (2019, June 21). *Are you a fan of astronomy? Enjoy reading about what scientists have discovered in our solar system – and beyond?* This [Image attached] [Status update]. Facebook. https://www.facebook.com/ScienceNOW/photos/a.117532185107/10156268057260108/?type=3&theater

Tweet:

Gates, B. [@BillGates]. (2019, September 7). *Today, it's difficult for researchers to diagnose #Alzheimers patients early enough to intervene. A reliable, easy and accurate diagnostic would* [Thumbnail with link attached] [Tweet]. Twitter. https://twitter.com/BillGates/status/1170305718425137152

As you can see, each type varies in the elements included, sequence of elements, and capitalization.

Types of lists

Check the assignment requirements so you provide the correct type(s) of citation list(s):

- **Reference list** All sources cited in the paper
- **Bibliography** All sources consulted when writing the paper, whether or not they are cited in the paper
- **Annotated bibliography** Bibliography with descriptions of each source.

Using a reference manager

If figuring out different reference formats seems intimidating, you will be glad to know there is a type of software that helps you get it right. Reference managers allow you to keep track of your references, and integrate with Microsoft Word or other word processing programs to generate reference lists. Applications include RefWorks, Zotero, Mendeley, and EndNote. Check your academic library because many have subscribed to a reference manager for their students' use.

Some reference managers work only within one document. These are too limiting, because you will have to keep entering source information when you reference this source again in other drafts or other writings. Look for one that allows you to store sources so you can add them into new documents as you continue to develop your academic writing.

 ACTIVITY Find and set up a reference manager

I   **Select a reference manager.** Look in your academic library to see whether a reference manager is offered. If so, download it. If they do not, look at RefWorks, Zotero, Mendeley, and/or EndNote and choose the one that best suits your style.

2   **Read or view any tutorials.**

3   **Set up the reference manager.** Keep in mind that the start-up phase does take some time, but the time-savings as you use it in future papers will be well worth your while.

A student told us

'Learning to use a reference manager is the single best step I've taken to save time and create citations and references in the proper format!'

Don't plagiarize!

First, let's address a fundamental issue: if our academic writing is based on flawed research or we are representing work as our own that is not, we can't accomplish our goals. We can't make an authentic contribution to our fields or make the world a better place. Once the truth comes out, ethical shortcomings make the news and reflect badly on the academy, scholarly research and publications. The repercussions at most institutions are quite harsh. Academic dishonesty may result in verbal or written disciplinary action. It may also result in your studies and support being terminated without an academic award. It will certainly result in the loss of your academic integrity.

We can't ignore the fact that we are in a tech-pervasive time when it is all too easy to simply cut and paste others' ideas. Popular 'mashup' culture blurs boundaries between acceptable and unacceptable use of others' work. Sometimes students cut and paste something and forget to cite it, or are just sloppy in the ways they reference materials they use. Other times, students intentionally cheat by copying or buying work they then submit as their own. See how these options look on a continuum that illustrates how these strategies correspond to degrees of honesty and originality.

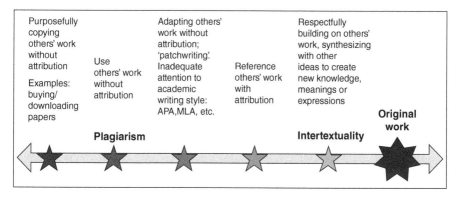

Figure 4.3 Continuum: from cheating to original work

On one side is intentional intellectual theft and misrepresentation. In the middle of this continuum you see the problems of ignorance or sloppy use of proper citations: issues that can be addressed by learning proper referencing, and/or using a reference manager.

The last point on the continuum takes you into new territory: plagiarism isn't simply inadequate use of citations, it represents *inadequate thinking*. From this perspective, while academic writers have sought to balance the desire to express new understandings in our own scholarly voices with expectations for situating that work within the literature of the field, the aspirational goal of academic research is not to produce papers with copious citations and clean reference lists. It is to generate insights and original thought that builds on past findings, sheds new light on the problems being investigated, and catalyzes action in the field of study or in practice. The absence of wrongdoing is still not enough. As you saw in Bloom's Taxonomy, the top tier of academic thinking is called *create,* which means contributing original insights.

When learning occurs online, institutions are even more concerned with plagiarism. Many have adopted **electronic detection tools** or search engine searches of suspicious phrases. Take care to avoid the appearance of plagiarism in your work. Here are a few key points to remember:

- When you are writing anything, you need to make sure you acknowledge the ideas you have collected and who you collected them from.

- All the work you present must be your own. It is not acceptable to submit someone else's work as yours when it isn't.

- It is not usually acceptable to rework all or part of work you have previously submitted in another course.

 Critique your writing

Look at a recent paper you have written.

1   Where on the continuum did your writing fall?

....

....

....

2   Were all sources cited?

....

....

....

3   Did you include your own analysis, evaluation, or insights?

....

....

....

4   What could you have done differently to improve originality of your thinking?

....

....

....

....

....

....

....

STAY FOCUSED

When most or all of your coursework occurs online, you have ample potential for distraction. Friends, social media, news updates: all call to us when we are trying to stay on task. The approaches suggested here often involve doing more than one thing at a time: you need to make notes while you read, you need to cite references when you write. Taking your mind off into unrelated paths will make it even more difficult to achieve excellence in your work.

 Next steps

Look at the activities from this chapter.

I   What did you learn about your reading, writing, and thinking styles?

....

....

....

2   How will you change your approach moving forward?

Use Bloom's Taxonomy to align work more precisely to assignment. ☐

....

....

....

Using a reference manager, pay attention to make sure all sources are cited? ☐

....

....

....

Review work to make sure you contributed original interpretations or insights? ☐

....

....

....

3   How can your approach to written work fit with the opportunities and limitations of online learning?

....

....

....

ASSIGNMENT CHECKLIST

The following checklist will help you to identify areas you need to think about before starting to write the assignment. Ensure you know how to:

Answer the question ☐

Create a logical, focused argument ☐

Provide evidence of independent research and reading ☐

Provide evidence of original ideas ☐

Present and maintain a clear structure ☐

Stick to the required guidelines ☐

Demonstrate accurate and appropriate use of language ☐

ESSAY PLANNING AND WRITING CHECKLIST

The following checklist will help you to identify areas you need to think about when planning and writing your essay. Ensure you know how to:

Identify requirements such as length and format ❑

Read the question carefully breaking it into parts or sub-questions ❑

Review the assignment using Bloom's Taxonomy ❑

Decide what evidence you need to know to answer each question ❑

Form the basic answers to the questions ❑

Critically read assigned textbooks and articles as well as your
independent research to find evidence to support your answers ❑

Take notes to show this evidence making sure to include source
information such as the author, book title, edition,
page number, URL, etc. ❑

Outline or otherwise plan out your structure making sure you set
and then answer each question in a logical order, and provide
your evidence ❑

Start writing, keeping your plan, notes and source materials at hand ❑

After you have written your assignment, use the checklist below.

Is the structure logical? ❑

Have you included adequate high-quality evidence? ❑

Is your presentation appropriate and clear? ❑

Have you used relevant literature in a fair and balanced way? ❑

Have you included your own ideas and original perspectives? ❑

Have you checked spelling and grammar? ❑

Have you checked punctuation? ❑

Have you read the essay out aloud? This will help you identify
any problems or errors. ❑

MILESTONE

CONGRATULATIONS!

You can analyse course requirements and prepare for assignments that ask you to conduct library or online research, critically read sources, and create academic papers that combine attention to sources and original thinking.

HOW DO I GET THE MOST FROM LEARNING WITH PEERS?

CHAPTER 5

60 second summary

Whether you are in a class that meets face-to-face, or a class that meets online, learning from others enriches the learning experience. Carrying out a discussion from a distance or working in online groups can seem intimidating, but if you approach the experience with an open mind, and understand what is involved in successful virtual collaboration, you might find peer interaction to be the most valuable part of your learning experience online. It can be a great way to learn, make new friends, and develop skills that will help in advanced academic study or professional life.

INTRODUCTION

Unless you are taking a self-paced tutorial, learning remotely doesn't mean you are learning alone. This chapter focuses on the ways students learn in an online class that involves peer interactions within a learning community. These interactions can relate to a single unit of study or occur across multiple weeks of a course.

Keep in mind that in all discussion and group assignments you are trying to demonstrate your mastery of the concepts of this course. That means you want to relate the ideas you present very clearly to course goals and objectives, and aim to demonstrate your ability to analyse, synthesize and apply the ideas presented in the readings and your own research on the topics at hand. See Chapters 3 and 4 for more about decoding learning goals and objectives.

Why is it important to learn together when studying online?

Learning together helps to reduce isolation. Rich interactions with peers and faculty break up the monotony you might feel when going to class means staring at a computer screen. Learning together allows for critical exploration of concepts from multiple perspectives. Hearing from others brings the subject matter to life. The key is open communication, a willingness to listen to others and actively acknowledge ideas, expertise, or skills that people can bring to the group.

When you learn together you develop skills you will need in a world where virtual teamwork is a necessity in most fields. As a learner today you will benefit from opportunities to develop 21st century skills that will allow you to work across boundaries of geography, time, and culture. Seismic shifts in the global workplace over the last decade show that operating in the age of the internet requires a different set of strategic, cross-cultural, team and technical skills than the face-to-face operations of the past. Leadership and teamwork are two key kinds of experiences that employers look for, and as an online learner you will be well prepared to succeed.

FIRST, DEFINE OUR TERMS

We will use the term *discussion* to describe interactions associated with topics and readings. These are probably single events, within a unit of study. In a discussion you are generally not trying to create a deliverable together.

Collaboration has become a buzzword, so the meaning can seem fuzzy. You might hear someone talk about collaborating with someone when they simply had a conversation with them. We are taking a much more specific use of the term. We will use the term *collaboration* to describe the processes we use to co-create ideas or products. *Collaborative e-learning* assignments, projects, presentations, or other deliverables that include contributions from more than one student. These kinds of activities typically cross more than one unit of study, multiple weeks, or can span the entire term.

KEY TERMS

Collaboration: an interactive process that engages two or more participants who work together to achieve outcomes they could not accomplish independently.

Collaborative e-learning: constructing knowledge, negotiating meanings and/or solving problems through mutual engagement of two or more learners in a coordinated effort using internet and electronic communications.

Two points stand out in this definition of collaborative e-learning:

- 'Mutual engagement, which means all are participating in shared, reciprocal work

- 'Coordinated effort', which means the project is purposeful and meshes with curricular goals.

How do we make sure everyone is engaged and contributing in a fair way? Whose responsibility is it to coordinate our efforts? We will try to answer those questions in this chapter and explore the roles of students and professors in making collaborative learning and interactive discussions thrive in your online class.

LEARNING FROM AND WITH EACH OTHER ONLINE

Learning online can feel isolating. You miss the social interaction of an in-person class, and there you are, alone with the computer. Learning together can alleviate some of that loneliness, but it also adds new challenges. Minor conflicts or miscommunication pitfalls can be magnified when we are working with others online, particularly when we don't know the other students or professor.

Throughout this book you have been encouraged to study course materials and listen carefully to your professor's explanation of assignments, course activities, and requirements. This is especially true when your success is reliant on others. Having a clear idea about what you are doing and why will help you determine how to approach the interactive part of your course. You will feel more confident and be able to get the most benefit from learning with your peers. And you will be the person everyone wants on their team!

Knowledge

Let's think about what we are trying to achieve and what our role(s) will be. Sometimes we have expertise to share, other times we need others' help. The Collaborative Knowledge Learning Model (Salmons, 2019) suggests four ways people may learn together:

- **Knowledge exchange** occurs when both of us have relevant knowledge on the topic, so we both share what we know.

- **Knowledge transfer** occurs when I know something you do not, so I share, guide, or coach you to transfer knowledge.

- **Knowledge acquisition** occurs when neither of us has relevant knowledge on the topic, so we acquire knowledge together.

- **Knowledge co-creation** occurs when we generate new knowledge together. Co-creation requires us to think together, innovate, negotiate meanings and/or solve problems.

It might not be obvious from the assignment what type of learning will occur. More often, these types emerge once we start working together and see where we fit in with others in the class, small group, or team. Are our backgrounds, experiences, interests, and previous exposure to the topics being studied similar or different? The roles aren't necessarily fixed: in the same project I might transfer knowledge to you on one occasion and another time you transfer knowledge to me.

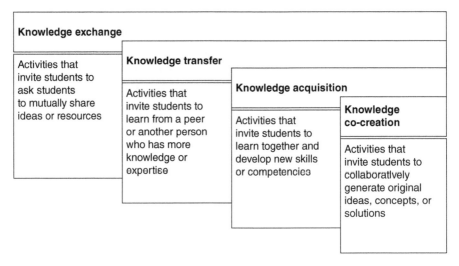

Figure 5.1 Learning from and with others

Being open to learning from and with each other requires that we are:

- **Self-aware** We realize our strengths and knowledge.

- **Generous** We are willing to share what we know, or resources we have that would help our peers.

- **Respectful of others** We are sensitive to the fact that peers might be reluctant to admit that they are ignorant about the topic, so we want to avoid seeming condescending. We realize that at other times we might need someone to transfer knowledge to us!

- **Open to new ideas** In order to acquire or co-create new knowledge, we must admit we don't know it all and the ways we have always done things are not necessarily the best.

- **Trustworthy** We can be relied upon to do what we commit to doing.

ACTIVITY Learning from and with each other

Imagine assignments or projects that would allow two students to use these ways of learning. Give one tip for students that would help them succeed in each example.

- Knowledge exchange
  - ○ Assignment or project: ....
    ....
    ....
  - ○ Tip for students: ....
    ....
    ....

- Knowledge transfer
  - ○ Assignment or project: ....
    ....
    ....
  - ○ Tip for students: ....
    ....
    ....

- Knowledge acquisition
  - ○ Assignment or project: ....
    ....
    ....

- o   Tip for students: ....

....

....

- • Knowledge co-creation
  - o   Assignment or project: ....

....

....

  - o   Tip for students: ....

....

....

Trust and online communication

You will need to trust me in order to be willing to participate in a knowledge transfer, and we need to trust each other if we are to be open to acquisition of new knowledge together. We need more trust and better communication as we move from simply sharing what we know to co-creating something new together. How do we develop a sense of mutual trust in an online class? There is no easy answer to this question, because other factors are at play.

To some extent human nature is a factor. Some people are more private, quiet and introverted, which can make it difficult to connect. Some approach groups with the mindset that they will trust others until proven otherwise, while others take the opposite view and must be convinced that they can trust you.

The personality of the professor and online teaching styles are factors. Some professors project warmth and create a class vibe that is open and friendly, and others do not. Is the culture of the class competitive or cooperative? The nature of the course is a factor – is the subject matter such that it has the potential to touch on sensitive personal experiences or divisive political or social issues? Table 5.1 offers some questions you can use to assess your own situation.

Table 5.1 Trusting students and the professor

Do I trust discussion or collaborative partners to:	Do I trust the professor:
• Listen, and respect what I have to say? • Be honest and forthcoming with me? • Ask for clarification if they are confused about something I said? • Carry out our agreements? • Honour confidentiality? • Be willing to resolve conflicts, even if that means involving the instructor or others in the educational institution?	• Was fair in the way that they designed the collaborative project, and assigned roles to students? • Will be available to help address problems that might arise?

These factors are out of your control as a student. What you *can* control is your own commitment to being honest and trustworthy. You can learn to set the limits you need to feel safe. You can also learn ways to establish agreements and accountability when you are working on a project with your peers.

 ACTIVITY **Assessing your class potential for peer learning and collaboration**

Assess factors in your class that could enable or obstruct your ability to learn from others. Ask yourself:

• What is the culture of the class?

• Are students from the same or different demographic groups or geographic area?

(Continued)

- Do you have prior relationships with peers from a face-to-face class or social life – or are they strangers to you?

- What level of trust do you feel about your professor and peers?

- What do you need in order to trust them enough to be able to participate in class learning activities?

- If not, what steps can you take to prepare yourself?

DISCUSSIONS

In most classes, discussion is a central part of the course. Online discussions can take a number of forms. They can be synchronous or asynchronous, or something in between. They can be informal or facilitated, flexible or required. The time-response factor in online communications was introduced in Chapter 1 and is relevant when considering how we hold discussions online.

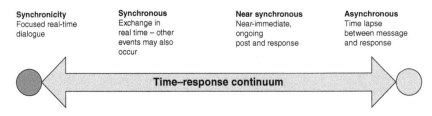

Figure 5.2 Time–response continuum

Synchronous discussions

Synchronous is the term used to describe ways of communicating at the same time. This means the professor and students are online together. Some situations call for *synchronicity*, that is, you are entirely focused on the discussion by minimizing other screens and avoiding multitasking. For example, for a discussion where your thoughtful and substantive participation is expected, you should close out other windows and reduce extraneous distractions. In a more informal check-in type of synchronous discussion, you could be more relaxed.

Advantages of synchronous discussions

- Immediate response

- Students can answer each other's questions, build on others' points

- Good for decision-making, where timely input and agreement are needed.

Disadvantages of synchronous discussions

- All must be online at the same time

- May require webcams, broadband or mics, which some students might not have.

Asynchronous discussions

Asynchronous is the term used to describe ways of interacting any time. There is typically a gap in time between the message or question and response. This means the professor and learners do not need to be online at the same time. On the time–response continuum you also see the option for *near-synchronous* communication. This indicates a shorter turnaround time. When you send a text message to someone you assume they will respond quickly, even if they are not able to respond in the moment. Whether it is asynchronous or near-synchronous, it is important to be clear about your expectations and communicate them. If you are communicating with a peer on a discussion or collaborative assignment that has a due date, you need to be sure you get a response within a defined timeline. A message such as, 'can you get back to me in two days?' lets your partner know what you need.

Advantages of asynchronous discussions

- No scheduling, works well when students are in diverse time zones
- Discussion organized by topic
- Messages can be any length
- Attachments are possible
- Responses are visible to all.

Disadvantages of asynchronous discussions

- Lacks spontaneity
- 'Low touch', i.e. harder to connect with others.

Asynchronous discussions typically take place on a private discussion board where the professor posts questions and students respond. Discussion boards are a common feature in LMSs, and there are also applications professors can adapt.

A common approach to asynchronous discussions in an online class has three parts:

1) Answer the question;
2) Respond to answers made by peers;
3) Review peer comments on your own answers.

As may be obvious, students need to answer the question in a timely way in order for fellow students to respond. It is important to follow the time sequence established by your professor.

Varied writing styles are possible, so you need to check the assignment guidelines or syllabus to understand your professor's expectations. Some online discussions are informal, based on personal reflection and sharing one's own experiences. Reflecting on your own experience is valuable for applying or testing what you are learning in the class. Synthesizing your own experiences with other concepts and theoretical constructs will enable you to grow intellectually and academically.

Other discussions are more formal, with answers presented using academic styles of writing, with citations and a reference list. When this is the case, incorporate ideas from the text, course readings, and your own research. Exercise critical thinking. Compare and contrast different examples, generalize from an example to larger principles that can be applied in other situations. Ask yourself, 'what is the larger significance of the point I am making?'

When responding to peers, provide thoughtful comments that build a sense of learning community and contribute to the value of the course for all learners. Treat other learners with respect and observe your institution's Code of Conduct.

Some classes might operate primarily with either synchronous or asynchronous modes, while others mix styles of interaction. Since synchronous scheduling can be an issue, live events can work well to launch or follow up on asynchronous discussions. For example, your professor could host a real-time session to introduce key concepts and answer questions, then use asynchronous tools for ongoing discussions or large or small group work. Or, they could start with asynchronous discussions and use the synchronous meeting for reporting out and summarizing key points.

 ## Synchronous and asynchronous discussions

I   What is one advantage and one disadvantage of communicating synchronously?

o   Advantage:

....

o   Disadvantage:

....

(Continued)

2   What is one advantage and one disadvantage of communicating asynchronously?

   o   Advantage:

   ....

   o   Disadvantage:

   ....

3   What is the difference between synchronicity and synchronous in online discussions?

   ....

   ....

   ....

4   What is the difference between asynchronous and near synchronous in online discussions?

   ....

   ....

   ....

5   How will you prepare to participate in online discussions of the type(s) included in your course?

   ....

   ....

   ....

COLLABORATIVE LEARNING ACTIVITIES

Collaborative learning activities are common in online learning. You might be assigned to a small group or dyad or be expected to form your own team. (For simplicity's sake, we will use the term *team* in this chapter.) You might be asked to collaborate on a written assignment, a research or practical project, or a presentation.

The purpose of the project, and of the people assembled to complete it, varies depending on whose idea it was. Did it originate from within the group or from the professor? In Chapter 1 we looked at the difference between instructional styles. This continuum will help you identify what student roles and level of autonomy there are for collaborative work in your course.

Collaboration does not mean leader-less. Particularly when communication is online – perhaps across time zones – decision-making and coordination will be needed. The professor might set the structure for the assignment, including appointing a leader, or leave it to your team. The team might decide to use different styles of leadership at different points. There might be times when you want to appoint someone as leader to move things along, and other times you want shared leadership so you can deliberate on how you want to proceed. Or you might want to rotate the role of project coordination on a longer project.

An agreement on team process is a must, whether or not it is required by the professor. Depending on the instructional style, you might fill in templates or follow the process steps your professor provides, work within guidelines, or develop your own approach to completing a collaborative assignment. With thoughtful upfront planning, you can succeed in any learning situation.

Plan to collaborate

Schedules and deadlines can make us feel that we should just jump in and get busy on the collaborative assignment. Or we may feel decisions about the content are more important than group process. However, making time to plan and agree to a collaborative process *before* we start the project can save precious hours in the long run.

Katzenbach and Smith, who have written several important books about teams, observe that a clearly understood charter, clear roles and areas of responsibility,

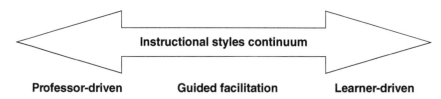

Professor-driven	Guided facilitation	Learner-driven
Lecture-oriented style	**Professor as facilitator**	**Professor as guide**
The professor defines the purpose and process of the collaborative assignment. They assign students to groups and might select leaders. They provide students with templates for the initial agreement and progress reports. Students focus on doing the project within set parameters.	The professor establishes the purpose and requirements of the project. Using frameworks from the professor, collaborative partners make their own agreements and determine leadership, decision-making, and establish how to monitor progress. The professor provides guidance or help if problems surface.	Students choose partners and determine the purpose and process for the project, within parameters set by the professor. Students make their own agreements. The professor provides guidance or help if problems surface.

Figure 5.3 Instructional styles continuum

and an understanding of accountability are critical factors for team success (Katzenbach and Smith, 2015). They outline some questions that can help teams clarify a working approach so the team can work smoothly to come to an agreement about how to proceed:

- Is the approach clear, understood and agreed upon by everyone?
- Will it capitalize on and enhance the skills of all members?
- Does it require all members to contribute equivalent amounts of work?
- Does it provide for open interaction, problem-solving and evaluation?
- Does it provide for modification and improvement?
- Are fresh input and perspectives sought and added?

Three important points should guide our discussion when we are getting started with a new team, particularly when working with a guided or learner-driven instructional style: agree to communicate, prepare for review, and make a plan.

1   Agree to communicate

Communication and trust are interrelated: we develop mutual trust when we understand each other. To succeed in a high-stakes project on an assignment that will affect your final grade, you need to think carefully about how, and how often, to communicate.

> 'A group becomes a team when each member is sure enough of himself and his contribution to praise the skills of others.'
>
> Norman Shidle

Take the time to affirm and celebrate others. Use inclusive and appropriately professional language in all cases.

In an online course the interactive process occurs electronically. Here are some questions to think about:

- Will you set checkpoints and hold meetings on a regular basis or just connect on an as-needed basis?

- When you send an email, what response time do you feel is appropriate? Who will be responsible for communicating with the professor if there is a problem?

- What document format(s) (Microsoft Word, PDF, HTML, PPTX) do you need to produce?

  o   What document format or academic style will you use?

  o   Can your software tools import and export these formats?

  o   Do you all have access to the same software?

- Will you use shared folders, or send drafts as email attachments? If you are in an LMS, is there a place to post work-in-progress files?

- Do you need to incorporate graphic files, data sets, or multimedia content into your work? Will these forms of content be embedded in your published work, or linked to it online?

- Do you ever need to work offline, or can everything 'live in the cloud'? If work is in the cloud, does everyone have broadband as needed to add and edit the files?

- How will you manage versions as the project evolves?

2   Prepare for review

Once team members have each completed a piece of the puzzle, the team will need to review each one in order to fit them together. How can you do this in a constructive and respectful way? Has the professor established quality standards for the completed project, or is it up to you to create them? If the professor has not set guidelines, discuss your process and agree to review criteria before you start looking at each other's work. Decide how you will work together to finalize the project. Trust is an important factor in the review stage. See Table 5.2. for questions to consider when thinking about trusting students and the professor in collaborative activities.

Table 5.2   Trusting students and the professor in collaborative activities

Do I trust discussion or collaborative partners to:	Do I trust the professor:
• Welcome my input and support my efforts as a contributor to this collaborative process?	• Has organized this collaborative assignment fairly?
• Give respectful feedback on my work, within your agreed-upon parameters?	• Will respond to questions or assist if problems surface?
• Avoid plagiarizing my work, including posting or forwarding work to others outside the group without my permission?	

3   Make a plan

Once you have decided how you will communicate, and what process you will use for assembling your contributions into one deliverable, you will want to spell it all out in a team charter and/or work plan. Here are a few process questions to consider:

- What leadership model will you use (one person leads, you rotate leadership, or share leadership)?

- How often will your team meet, and in what way will you meet? Synchronous or asynchronous?

- What parts of the project will you complete individually, and what work will you complete together?

- What ground rules will your team develop?
- How will you communicate with each other?

Following are some examples you can adapt to fit your collaborative project. They include professor-driven, facilitated, or learner-driven learning situations.

Learner-driven *plan*

In this situation, the team works within broad guidelines provided by the professor, but determines the format and steps. That means you have to determine the process you will use, as well as doing the assignment itself.

As a team, spell out your answers in a 2–4-page agreement.

- How will you learn and work together to co-create the assignment?
- What leadership model will you use (fixed, rotating, shared)?
- What parts of the project will you complete individually, and what work will you complete together?
- How often will your team meet, and in what way will you meet?
- What ground rules will your team develop?
- How will you communicate with each other?

Planning with the professor's guidance

In this situation the professor outlines what should be included in the team agreement. When you are reviewing their guidance, use this list to make sure you have all the information you will need.

1 **Clarify how you will co-create the assignment**
- What are the required project phases and steps?
- What are the deliverables?

- What are the deadlines and due dates?

- What steps can or should be completed by team members individually?

- What steps can or should be completed by team members as a group?

2   **Clarify expectations that team members have for themselves and the project**

- What skills and knowledge does the team have? Will you exchange, transfer, or acquire the skills and knowledge needed to co-create the assignment? Who will provide help and leadership on specific tasks and assignments? Who would like to try something new or different? What outside resources do team members have that might help the project team?

- What would members like to get out of the process? What are each person's specific learning objectives? What benefits could be gained from the project? What concerns and questions do members have?

- How will you communicate progress and finalize the deliverables?

- How will coordination and reporting duties be handled?

- What will be the consequences if a team member does not complete his/her assignments promptly?

3   **Prepare the team agreement**

- Establish ground rules to foster a positive team climate.

- Distribute or post a team roster including phone numbers, email addresses, and other contact information.

- Brainstorm the activities required to produce each deliverable.

- Divide up the work.

- Prepare a work plan.

Professor provides an agreement template

It takes time to go through the decision-making entailed by the first two examples. Your professor might decide to just create a template that all teams use.

The professor might also appoint a leader to help organize the process. After a short planning process, teams focus their time on completion of the project. Here is a template example.

Table 5.3 Agreement template

Team charter template
Team members:
Names, roles, etc.
Operating logistics:
Ground rules:
Deliverables:
Membership responsibilities:
Project work plan:
Key milestones:
Detailed tasks:

REFLECT ON YOUR ROLE

You might think of learning from and with peers as a group endeavour, yet the role and responsibility of each individual is critical. As individuals, we each need to believe that the process is fair and that our ideas are valued. We need to reflect on the assets (and shortcomings) we bring to the group. If we don't know what we want and hope from our peers, how can we expect them to meet our expectations? Taking time to reflect allows us to make sense of what we are learning from the interactive discussion or collaborative project.

Checklist for working with peers

You may have to take on a role outside your comfort zone – try to focus on the positives of learning new skills. Don't be afraid to ask for help if you get stuck. ❑

Give people time to think before expecting a response. Listen or re-read before you respond – respond, don't over-react! ❑

Consider how you might express disagreement with someone without appearing confrontational. It is important to express disagreements in a positive, constructive, professional way. ❑

> 'Alone we can do so little; together we can do so much.'
>
> Helen Keller

CHECK POINT

Got it?

Why should I take the time to make agreements and communication plans, when I could just do the assignment myself?

Got it!

Isolation is bridged, online learning is enriched, when we interact with peers.

HOW DO I GET THE MOST FROM ASSESSMENTS AND FEEDBACK?

CHAPTER 6

60 second summary

To get a good grade in an online class, be clear on expectations and requirements. Ask questions on anything you don't understand. It is essential to understand the assessment process instructors typically use in online learning. You might think that assessment means being graded on your work, but in online learning it is usually a more complex process. You might be asked to assess yourself and assess others, and in the process your work will be assessed. It is time to be prepared to take an active role and learn more (and get the best grade)!

INTRODUCTION

Why is assessment different in an online class? If a face-to-face class meets on Tuesday at 1pm, everyone is there at that time. Presentations, discussions, and participation in group activities happens then and the professor can see that you are there and engaged. You know that you need to prepare before Tuesday to get ready. In an online class a synchronous discussion can take place over a week or more. You have more flexibility, but you also need to have more self-discipline to make sure you have set aside time to participate. As you saw in Chapter 3, online discussions can have multiple stages in which to answer and respond to others' posts.

Larger papers and projects might be due at the end of the term so, again, you need to use good management to complete reading, writing, and proofreading in a timely fashion. You might also need some checkpoints and feedback along the way, including feedback from peers as well as the professor. This is where assessment comes into play – and a reason why it is critical to know how assessment works. Ideally, assessment is:

- **Timely**: with adequate turnaround so you can integrate input into the next assignments

- **Explicit**: everyone understands the expectations – learners and professor
- **Systematic**: grading is fair and congruent with expectations as stated in course goals and learning objectives.

To avoid confusion, here are some basic definitions for terms used in this chapter. Broadly, *assessment* describes processes used to determine the success of learners in achieving learning goals. The term *outcomes* refers to the deliverables (such as papers or presentations) as well as to measurable learning (such as improved knowledge, skills, or abilities) that result from your studies.

While assessment is sometimes used interchangeably with the word *evaluation*, this term typically refers to processes used to determine success of the programme, curriculum, or course. In other words, in this context the institution might evaluate the course to determine whether the textbook needs to be updated, but a professor assesses the students.

With planning and mutual accountability, assessment can become an avenue for meaningful communication – essential when we are working remotely!

FIRST, GO BEHIND THE SCENES

Look behind the curtain to understand how the course design relates to expectations for learners. Your first task is to fully understand interrelated course goals, learning objectives, and measures that will be used to determine whether you have demonstrated mastery of the course material in your completed assignments and learning activities. You might notice that some aspects of your performance will count more than others. For example, in one course exams might count for a larger percent of the grade, in another research papers or essays count more.

Courses are designed to fit within your academic programme. You need to achieve some competence in this course, so you are prepared for the next course and, at the end, a degree. The level of competence will be spelled out in course goals. The goals might be embedded into the course description, or in a separate section. These larger goals are broken down into measurable learning objectives (also known as learning outcomes). Learning objectives might be listed under a heading such as 'By the end of the course, students should be able to'. The objectives guide the criteria used to determine whether the work you did on a particular assignment meets expectations.

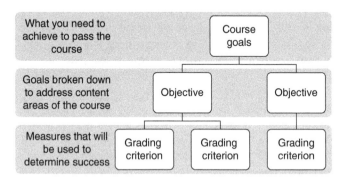

Figure 6.1 Mapping from general goals to specific measures

What assessment tools will be used in this course?

Your course might have been designed in a few different ways.

- The professor created a conventional course, then moved it online.
- The professor created an online course.
- A team of instructional designers, online learning specialists, and subject matter experts collaborated on the development of the course.

Depending on your institution's approach, as described in Chapter 1, the course might have been designed to work within a Learning Management System (LMS) and use its set of features. An LMS has automated digital tools and rubrics for assessment that we will explore in this chapter. Alternatively, the course might have been developed for use with an *à la carte* collection of technologies selected by the institution or the professor, including applications for assessment. Finding and familiarizing yourself with the assessment tools is an important step in your process.

Learn to work for success!

Looking only at the grading information without looking at the whole context would be like looking at a cake recipe starting with the stage of putting it into the oven, without looking at the part that explains the ingredients and how they should be combined. Let's start from the beginning and see how it all fits together!

 Find out how you will be assessed

1   Scan the course syllabus and any other course guidance. Find course goals, objectives, requirements, grading breakdown, and any other explanations about how your professor will handle grading and/or assessing progress.

2   Copy goals, objectives, and grading breakdown into a new document so you can analyse them as you work through this chapter.

3   Identify the digital tools being used in this course to record and/or share grades and feedback.

BLOOM'S TAXONOMY REVISITED

Now that you have found the course goals, objectives, and criteria, look closely at the action keywords. They will clue you into what, specifically, you need to focus on to meet the grading criteria. Bloom's Taxonomy was introduced in Chapter 4. This tool is commonly used by colleges and universities as a guideline for articulating learning objectives. When you look at objectives or grading criteria with this taxonomy as a lens, you can see more clearly what you are expected to achieve.

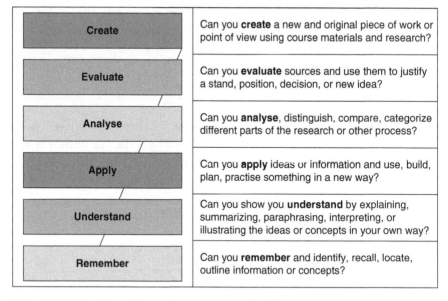

Create	Can you **create** a new and original piece of work or point of view using course materials and research?
Evaluate	Can you **evaluate** sources and use them to justify a stand, position, decision, or new idea?
Analyse	Can you **analyse**, distinguish, compare, categorize different parts of the research or other process?
Apply	Can you **apply** ideas or information and use, build, plan, practise something in a new way?
Understand	Can you show you **understand** by explaining, summarizing, paraphrasing, interpreting, or illustrating the ideas or concepts in your own way?
Remember	Can you **remember** and identify, recall, locate, outline information or concepts?

Figure 6.2   Using Bloom's Taxonomy to understand performance expectations

 ACTIVITY Assessing different kinds of student performance

How would you assess the extent to which a student's work succeeded with each level of learning? What would you look for? Give it a try with this activity.

How would determine whether a student could:

Remember

Understand

Apply

Analyse

Evaluate

Create

Could you use this process to review your own work before you submit it?

FEEDBACK AND GRADES

There are two ways professors let you know how you are doing: formative and summative assessments; in short, feedback and grades. Formative assessment can be verbal or written, whereas summative assessment is usually a quantitative measure.

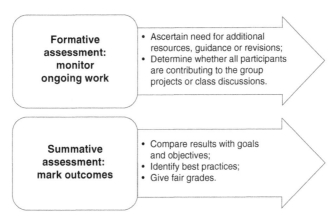

Formative assessment: monitor ongoing work
- Ascertain need for additional resources, guidance or revisions;
- Determine whether all participants are contributing to the group projects or class discussions.

Summative assessment: mark outcomes
- Compare results with goals and objectives;
- Identify best practices;
- Give fair grades.

Figure 6.3   Formative and summative assessment

Formative assessment is the term used for the feedback that lets you know whether or not you are heading in the right direction and making progress. It provides you with information about how to improve performance. In an online course where you might be working on a paper or project over a period of time, feedback is extremely important. Take advantage of any opportunity for feedback, whether in submission of an outline or draft, or an office hour consultation.

Summative assessment describes the process your professor uses to gather evidence needed to assign grades. It is their judgement which encapsulates how your work measures up, given all the evidence up to a specific point.

RECEIVING FEEDBACK

Keep in mind that the kinds of written comments you will experience online can seem more critical than those offered verbally. Lacking tone of voice, facial expresssions and other non-verbal signals means a simple statement could be misinterpreted. Avoid jumping to conclusions.

Professor: This draft needs work. (I really mean, you are off to a good start, keep going!)

Student: Oh no! I am going to fail the class!

Figure 6.4 The professor says...   **Figure 6.5** The student hears...

It can be really difficult to engage with feedback from your first few assignments because it can feel as though you are being reprimanded. As we are not always used to receiving feedback and written advice, however gently it is given, it can still feel like a personal attack when you receive it. Try not to take it personally as it is not usually directed at you but remember it is meant as guidance to help you progress and get better marks next time.

Don't be afraid to ask!

If the comment is unclear, ask for more detail. Reaching out to your professor can be intimidating in an online class. You might feel that you alone are perplexed by an assignment, but that is highly unlikely. More than likely if you have a question so do your peers! If you have a general assessment-related question, ask in a synchronous session or post in the asynchronous discussion area. Most online professors would rather answer your questions and feel confident you understand what is expected, than see an incomplete or off-base submission.

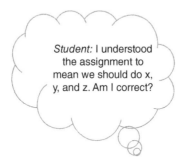

Figure 6.6   Ask for clarification, and do it early

You can take the initiative and ask for some formative assessment if it is not formally offered in the course. Pose a specific question, not a general "help!" Instead of sending a lengthy draft for preliminary review, send or share a section and ask whether the style and substance are appropriate. Similarly, if you have questions about a grade, or the process to be used for grading, request clarification.

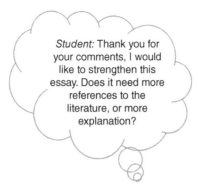

Figure 6.7   Ask for details as needed

TIP There are few things that aggravate professors more than this behaviour: after taking the time to make extensive comments on a paper, the student submits it without making changes as indicated. If you disagree with their perspective, discuss why you chose not to make suggested changes. But simply ignoring feedback will be seen as a sign of disrespect.

TIP Ask for help or suggestions early – don't wait until the last minute, when your professor is fielding lots of questions. This is why the activities in this chapter should be undertaken at the beginning of a new course.

TIP Whether you want more guidance about work in progress or clarification about a grade, be respectful and keep in mind that your professor is busy. Identify specific questions. Ask for an appointment if you want verbal comments or a chance to discuss a problem. Most importantly, use what you learn to improve your performance.

 Make sure you know how you will be assessed!

Look at the syllabus and any course documents again. Highlight the assessments that are part of the class.

- Does the course include both formative and summative assessments?
- If summative assessments are not offered, are there points in the term when you want feedback on your progress?
- If so, identify your communication strategy and make a plan to contact your professor.

ASSESSING INDIVIDUALS, TEAMS, OR GROUPS

So far, we have explored assessment of your own work. Of course, in most online courses you are engaged in discussions, projects, presentations, and/ or other kinds of learning with and from your peers. (See Chapter 5 for more on peer learning.) This means you are likely to experience at least one form of individual and collective assessment.

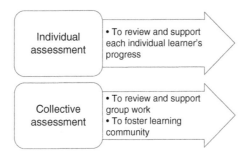

Figure 6.8 Individual assessment of your work, collective assessment of the group's work

It is not uncommon to expect self-assessment and peer assessment as well as assessment by the professor. In online classes that include field work or practical, external supervisors may also provide assessment. Let's look at each type and what it means for you.

Table 6.1 Typology of assessments (Salmons, 2019)

Typology of e-learning assessment	
Type	**Description**
1 Self-assessment (individual)	Individual self-assessment takes place when the learner provides his or her own assessment of performance.
2 Self-assessment (collective)	Collective self-assessment takes place when the team or group assesses their combined performance.
3 External assessment (individual)	When a project or placement extends beyond the classroom, external supervisors, mentors or stakeholders may assess the learner's performance.
4 External assessment (collective)	When a collaborative or team project or activity extends beyond the classroom, external supervisors, mentors or stakeholders may assess the team or group's performance.
5 Instructor assessment (individual)	The instructor assesses individual achievement.

(Continued)

Table 6.1 (Continued)

Typology of e-learning assessment	
Type	**Description**
6 Instructor assessment (collective)	The instructor assesses collective outcome according to the achievement of the entire group.
7 Grading	The instructor uses numerical or alphabetical scores to communicate a quantitative measure of success in relation to stated goals and standards.

Self-assessment

Self-assessment is important any time, but absolutely necessary when you are learning online. You need to be able to double-check your work before submitting it, because you are representing yourself to peers, and the professor with your work. With the goals, objectives, keywords from Bloom's Taxonomy at hand, look at your work with a critical eye – before you post or send it for others' review. Taking this kind of care, avoiding the need for review of sloppy or poorly written work, shows respect for others.

At the same time, self-assessment allows you to be mindful of your own learning and personal and academic growth. If the coursework does not offer a formal self-assessment component, consider keeping a reflective journal.

Another option is to track your assessments across courses. It can sometimes be hard to see patterns in the feedback your professors and peers give, but if you use a table to record your reflections and observations, you will be able to see similar themes that arise in the comments you get. There may be one thing you're doing – or not doing – that means you're not performing as expected. Spotting it will help you avoid repeated disappointments by working on a long term fix or getting help with a specific skill.

Track and plan to use feedback

Using Table 6.2, log feedback from a current or past assignment, and plan next steps to strengthen your performance.

Table 6.2 Assessment tracker

Course/module	Assignment name	Summary of feedback	Next steps

Collective self-assessment

When you are part of a team or group assignment or discussion, think about ways to build self-assessment into collaborative work. This can take the form of an informal discussion of progress and next steps. You might be asked to submit an interim report, or a more formal review of status in relation to plans for completion. Your initial team agreements or charter can help structure this kind of review.

To complete a collective self-assessment you might be asked to review the work of your peers. This can be disconcerting in an online environment, particularly when you have not had a chance to develop personal rapport and trust with others in the class. Stick with the parameters set by the instructor or in your agreement with your fellow student. For example, if you are asked to review a draft for accuracy, but were not asked to review the grammar, omit such comments. Alternatively, ask your peer whether they would like feedback on writing as well as content, or not.

When giving peer feedback, especially negative feedback, be specific and cite particular evidence. If the problem rouses an emotional response on your part, step aside and calm down. Think about the kind of feedback you would like to receive! Where changes are needed, be specific. Keep these three stages in mind:

1   Identify the specific error. For example: 'the reference for virtual teamwork on page 2 seems outdated.'

2   Describe the impact of the behaviour on the learner's performance, grade, potential impact, as appropriate. For example: 'The professor mentioned that all references related to technology need to be less than five years old. You don't want to lose grade points on this source!'

3   Give explicit information or direction about what needs to change and whether you want a revision of the assignment or improvement on the next one. For example: 'In the final team report, you might want to reference Jones (2020) for this point. I'll share a link to the article.'

Don't assume you are right – in some circumstances it is worthwhile to give your peer a chance to explain or give a rationale for their choice. In the example above, you could add: 'Is there a reason why you are referencing a source from

1999? If this writer was a trailblazer who changed the field, please explain. If not, consider my suggestion for a current source.'

External assessment

As noted in Chapter 2, when you are studying online, you can cross boundaries for internships, fieldwork or observations, volunteer or service-learning projects. If you do so, expect that someone associated with that placement will probably have some assessment responsibility for your efforts, and/or the accomplishments of your team. The challenge in such situations can be that people in non-academic workplaces might have very different expectations about feedback and assessment. Make sure expectations are well defined for the project and level of completion. For example, is your student team developing a template for the NGO's newsletter, or writing the newsletter? If communication channels are not established, facilitate a discussion with your professor and external supervisor.

Table 6.3 Individual and collective assessment from different sources

	Formative assessment: comments, suggestions and recommendations	Summative assessment: grading, marks, and review notes
Individual assessment	*Self-assessment* Careful proofreading and editing Journal or portfolio entries	*Self-assessment* Critique of own performance including process, contributions, and outcomes
	External assessment Feedback about progress and suggestions for improvement from service-learning, internship, or field placement supervisor	*External assessment* Review of performance at completion of field placement
	Professor's assessment Comments on individual work (or individual contributions to group work) with explanation of improvements needed to meet expectations	*Grading* Marks and grades in the form of numerical or letter score

(Continued)

Table 6.3 (Continued)

	Formative assessment: comments, suggestions and recommendations	Summative assessment: grading, marks, and review notes
Collective assessment	*Self-assessment* Team progress report Update to charter or workplan Summary of work process	*Professor's assessment* Review of collective contributions and achievement by the group
	External assessment Feedback to team by field placement supervisor	*External assessment* Review of field project
	Instructor assessment Written or verbal feedback; troubleshooting on team process or group performance	*Grading* Numerical or letter score representing group participation or outcomes

 ACTIVITY What kinds of assessment do you prefer?

1 Given your own personal and learning styles, what kind(s) of self-assessment do you use when you have a choice?

2 How does self-assessment help you strengthen and improve your work?

3 Think about situations where you have received peer feedback. How would you characterize that feedback? Was it effective?

4 How can you provide constructive feedback to peers, especially when you are in a team or group project together?

GRADING

Students want to receive the best marks possible! For some students, funding, support, or degree completion can depend on the grade-point average. As noted, many online classrooms on LMS platforms have automated gradebooks that allow you to view your grade as it evolves throughout the term.

If you do not have access to a gradebook of this kind, it might be your responsibility to keep track of grades on submissions so you are aware if a problem arises. Using Table 6.4, or your own system, start keeping a regular record of the grades you achieve for your assignments.

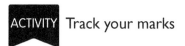 Track your marks

Use Table 6.4 or create your own system for tracking grades.

Table 6.4 Grade tracker

Course/ module	Assignment title and type	Feedback from professor or peers	Grade or mark	Areas where I can improve

Scoring rubrics

Whether it is part of the LMS or not, one way that professors communicate expectations and differentiate levels of work is through the use of rubrics. Rubrics are tables with the assessment criteria in one column, and criteria for different levels of performance in the other columns. See Figure 6.9 for the defining characteristics of a rubric.

Scoring rubrics	Convey expectations for the assignment
	Distinguish levels of performance
	Differentiate more critical and less critical aspects of student work
	Ensure consistent grading across the class
	Provide a framework for developing comments

Figure 6.9 Defining characteristics of grading rubrics

You might receive Word or Excel rubrics with the syllabus, the assignment description, or with your graded assignment. If you do not see it, asking your professor whether rubrics will be used is not inappropriate. Two examples are offered here for the kinds of rubrics you might encounter: a comment rubric and a scoring rubric.

Comment rubric

A comment rubric combines formative and summative assessments. This example is for team formation, so would be a collective type of assessment. You can see in the *criteria* column how the points are allocated across parts of the assignment, and points received in the *score* column. In this example, 12 points are the maximum for perfect mastery of all criteria. Comments and suggestions are offered in the middle column. It should be obvious what this team needs to do to receive a maximum mark on this assignment.

Table 6.5 Example of a comment rubric with allocation of points

Criteria	Comments	Score
Provides a project charter that indicates clear role definitions and responsibilities **(4 points)**	Roles are clearly defined. Communication responsibilities are not spelled out. If everyone can't participate in the conference call, will you post outcomes of the call so others can weigh in?	3
Outlines tasks for completion of team project **(2 points)**	Tasks for each stage of work are listed with due dates.	2
Provides specifics of the logistics, ground rules, and milestones **(4 points)**	Work plans are presented. Expectations are stated. Ground rules are clear and specific.	4
Provides a project charter that indicates team members reflected on their skills and development areas **(2 points)**	I see that you have not specifically identified team skill goals. Did your team discussion discuss how the roles you are taking will allow you to build new skills in team leadership and team participation? Can you post your thoughts about this?	1
12 points	Please re-submit your team charter with revisions as noted.	10 points

Scoring rubric

A scoring rubric typically has five columns that spell out what is needed to succeed at each level, from unsatisfactory to excellent. Again, the criteria column shows the grading emphasis.

CHECKLIST FOR ASSIGNMENT FEEDBACK

If your professor offers rubrics for marking assignments, download and review them. ❏

If your professor does not offer rubrics for marking assignments, look at any criteria that are posted for marking. ❏

Make notes about the areas of emphasis. Make notes about any additional steps, such as library research, you will need to complete in order to complete the assignment at the *excellent* level. ❏

When a rubric or other description of grading criteria is available for your assignments, you can use it for self-assessment prior to submission of your work. You can make sure key requirements are covered and address any shortcomings to improve your grade.

YOU ARE READY TO LEARN AND SUCCEED!

Now you have a full understanding of what is expected of you in this course, and what you can ask for if you need clarification, feedback, or guidance. You are able to work with groups or teams virtually, to aim together for top performance. You know how to learn from shortcomings and move forward.

'Success does not consist in never making mistakes but in never making the same one a second time.'

George Bernard Shaw

Putting it all together

Look at the activities from this chapter. Ask yourself:

1 What did you learn about your course?

....

....

....

....

2 How will you change your approach to individual assignments to get the marks you want?

....

....

....

....

3 How will you change your approach to team or group assignments to get the marks you want?

....

....

....

....

Checklist for achieving top marks

Use this checklist to make sure you understand what you need to achieve top marks:

Review course goals and learning objectives. ☐

Look for action keywords associated with Bloom's Taxonomy and make notes about what they mean for completion of assignments, papers, projects, discussions and/or teamwork in this course. ☐

Find out what types of assessment the professor offers: ☐

o   Formative feedback?

o   Summative marks?

Identify ways to get the feedback you need. ☐

Find out whether you are expected to use self-assessment.

o   If yes, in what form?

o   If no, do you want to create your own tracking or assessing tables, journals, or other systems?

Reflect on how you will receive and address feedback. ☐

If the course involves a group or team project, investigate how collective assessment will work. ☐

Reflect on how you will give feedback to peers. ☐

Attribute all sources and avoid plagiarism. ☐

Look for rubrics or other ways the professor spells out grading criteria. ☐

Don't panic! You can do it! ☐

MILESTONE

CONGRATULATIONS!

You can now understand and evaluate your course requirements and assessment protocols and be ready to exceed expectations!

HOW DO I MOVE FORWARD?

CHAPTER 7

60 second summary

You need to take the practical steps described throughout this book. You also need an open mind, a willingness to learn, a place to study, and the tools for connecting online.

In the previous chapters you have had a chance to reflect on your styles and skills, and to explore some of the kinds of course activities you can expect in an online course. In this chapter you will look at the practical preparations for learning online.

INTRODUCTION

Learning online means you are not going to a physical classroom; you are studying in a place of your choosing. Learning online means you are using digital tools to connect. Learning online means you are expected to be able to work independently. These facts mean you are responsible for organizing your own learning environment. In this chapter we will walk through some of these practical steps.

SETTING UP YOUR ONLINE LEARNING STUDY SPACE

When we think of an online learning study space, we need to consider the physical location as well as the digital set-up. Let's look at setting up a study space and preparing for mobile study. Then we will consider some hardware and software essentials for your digital set-up.

Setting up your study office

In Chapter 1 you saw that all online learning is not the same. If you are taking online courses, but your degree programme is based primarily on a physical campus, your physical set-up might be different. You might have access to a campus setting such as a library where you can study and write.

Ideally, establish a dedicated study space. If study is the main activity in that corner of your world, you will get into the study mindset when you sit at that table or desk. Make it a place where you are at ease and ready to put your attention to your coursework. Make sure your chair is comfortable and that you have adequate lighting.

If it is not feasible to have a private dedicated space in your home, apartment, or dormitory, is there another place where you can go to have a quiet study area? If your online learning is the blended style, you might be able to access the university library; if not, does your local library have reading areas? Is there a co-working space where you can reserve a study area? If possible, a consistent location will help set the mood to the focused attention needed for online learning. If not, make your mobile set-up one that allows you to be in study mode wherever you are.

Minimize distractions

From social media to doing the dishes to friends wanting to chat, you'll be tempted by distractions that can easily derail your studies. The best online students are disciplined about lessening these distractions and set aside time to focus. The deep reading and critical thinking necessary to complete papers and assignments, the attention needed to focus on your professor's lecture or meeting, require you to tune out other matters. Working independently can make this more difficult. If you were in a face-to-face setting it would be obvious if you started watching a television show or got up in the middle of the class to make lunch. Online, no one is there to look askance. It is up to you, and you will need to find a strategy that works best in your circumstances.

Regardless of where you choose to work, turn your cell phone off to avoid shifting your attention every time a text message or notification pops up. If you find your social media accounts irresistible, try a website blocker. Some programmes such as Word have a 'focus' setting, or you can download an application for that purpose. If this seems too restrictive, refer to the time management section in Chapter 1, and use a system such as Pomodoro that shows you how to set up timing for focus and breaks.

Keeping track of your materials

If your textbooks and course materials are all digital, little actual space will be needed. You will just need your laptop and essential items that can live in your dedicated space and/or your backpack.

If you have paper textbooks, as well as reference books, writing or dissertation/ thesis guides, find a shelf or safe place where they can stay between study sessions. We saw in Chapter 2 that some people enjoy the tactile nature of paper and analog writing instruments, in conjunction with electronic tools. If that is the case for you, consider a paper journal where you can make notes and lists. A bound journal will mean everything is in one place, and little bits of paper (with critical phone or page numbers) will not escape.

If you prefer to print out articles, create a file system that means you won't need to search through piles to find what you need. If you do not have a filing cabinet, consider using binders to keep printed articles organized by topic, course, or publication year. This point is especially relevant for those who will be writing a thesis or dissertation and will need to be able to keep track of literature.

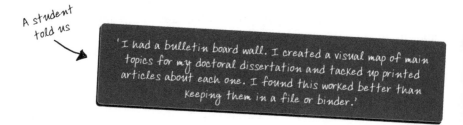

A student told us

'I had a bulletin board wall. I created a visual map of main topics for my doctoral dissertation and tacked up printed articles about each one. I found this worked better than keeping them in a file or binder.'

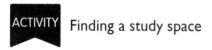

Finding a study space

To succeed in online learning you will need a place to study. Using the guidance described in this book, make a plan:

Do you have study space at home?.. Y/N

Can you access study space in a library or community location?.. Y/N

Steps I will take to make a study space distraction-free as possible:

1 ....

....

2 ....

....

3 ....

....

YOUR MOBILE STUDY KIT

You might need the flexibility to study anywhere so you'll want a to-go study kit. This should include your digital tools and software, and other items that will help you stay organized.

Digital tools

When you are learning online you will want a laptop computer. Locate the computer requirements document on the university or course website and make sure your computer fits the requirements. While some interactions can be accomplished on a mobile phone or tablet, digital library research and research papers will be difficult to manage without a keyboard. Being able to participate in a videoconference presentation or meeting, while having relevant documents and note-taking pages on your desktop, requires a bigger monitor than mobile devices offer.

In addition to a computer, a headset is a must. You will need headphones for listening to lectures or discussions (especially important in shared spaces). If possible, select headphones that include a microphone, for better sound quality. Even if your computer has a built-in mic, it will pick up any background noise, which will be disruptive to the videoconference lecture or meeting. A more expensive item is a set of noise-cancelling headphones, which could be worth the investment if you are going to study in places where noise and conversations are inescapable.

The third piece of hardware you will need is a webcam. Most contemporary laptops have built-in webcams, but desktops typically do not. You will want to build social presence by showing your face in online class meetings.

Once you have a computer, headset, and webcam, make sure they all work! Test them out before you join a meeting. One step that seems to catch out many people is the ability to mute and unmute the microphone. Be prepared to mute when you are not speaking, and quickly unmute when you are.

Of course, you cannot connect without internet. It will be difficult to use most online learning LMSs or videoconferencing platforms without a high-speed or broadband internet connection. If possible, choose a plan that allows for unlimited access.

Software and applications

In terms of software, you will most likely need:

- Microsoft Word, Apple Pages, or Google Docs for writing papers
- Microsoft PowerPoint, Apple Keynote, or Google Slides for presentations
- Adobe Acrobat or Corel Fusion for reading and creating PDFs.

Depending on your field of study, you might need other specialized database, drawing, or technical software.

Some schools provide software as downloads from their bookstore, technical support page, or library, so check availability before you buy software. If you plan to purchase a new computer or software, check your university or college bookstore to see whether discounts are available to students. If not, look online. There are technology distributors that specialize in academic sales and discounts can be significant.

Other apps and tools for student success

There are plenty of apps around to help you plan for academic success, whether they help you with referencing, note-taking or staying organized. You will want to choose a bibliographic manager for referencing (see Chapter 3). Before making a selection, check your academic library to see if they support one and offer it free to students.

Table 7.1 Software applications for student success

App	Available on	Free or paid?	How does it help?	Category
Be Focused	iOS	Free	Helps you make use of the 'Pomodoro' time-management method	Time management
Focus Booster	Mac/PC	Free and paid	Helps you make use of the 'Pomodoro' time-management method	Time management
SelfControl	iOS	Free	Allows you to blacklist or whitelist distracting websites for a set period of time	Motivation
Evernote	Android/ iOS/PC	Free and paid	Offers a range of ways to take notes – type, draw, record audio and video, etc. and access them across computers or devices	Note-taking

(Continued)

Table 7.1 (Continued)

App	Available on	Free or paid?	How does it help?	Category
OneNote	Android/ iOS/PC	Installed on Windows	Offers a range of ways to take notes – type, draw, record audio and video, etc. and access them across computers or devices	Note-taking
SimpleMind	Android/ iOS/PC	Free and paid	Digital mind-mapping tool that lets you note-take in a visual way	Note-taking
Dropbox	Android/ iOS/PC	Free	Cloud-based file hosting and sharing app that allows you to store your files safely	Organization
Google Drive	Android/ iOS/PC	Free	Cloud-based file hosting and sharing app that allows you to store your files safely and work collaboratively	Organization
OneDrive	Android/ iOS/PC	Free and paid, installed on Windows	Cloud-based file hosting and sharing app that allows you to store your files safely and work collaboratively	Organization
Todoist	Android/ iOS/PC	Free and paid	Works on and offline to help you keep track of tasks	Organization
Cite This For Me	Android/ iOS/PC	Free	Helps you create a reference list in any of the main citation styles	Referencing
EasyBib	Android/ iOS	Free and paid	Helps you create a reference list in any of the main citation styles	Referencing
EndNote	Android/ iOS/PC	Paid	Create libraries of references and cite-as-you-write	Referencing
Zotero	Android/ iOS/PC	Free	Helps you create a reference list in any of the main citation styles	Referencing
StudyBlue	iOS/ Android	Free	Allows you to create electronic flashcards and practice quizzes	Revision
Oxford Dictionary	Android/ iOS	Free	Offers a quick reference guide for spelling and grammar	Spelling and grammar

Salmons, J. (2019) *Learning to collaborate, collaborating to learn: Engaging students in the classroom and online.* Sterling: Stylus.

Items for organization

Simple and inexpensive items can save time and aggravation. For example, papers in classic manilla folders will inevitably fall out in your backpack – or all over the coffee shop floor. If you have paper documents or notes, purchase folders with closures and set up one for each course.

A multi-plug is a must-have so you can plug in your computer and charge your mobile phone in places where everyone is trying to do the same thing and outlets are limited.

 Assemble your mobile study kit

Create your checklist and indicate what you have and what you need to acquire.

Digital tools

✓ Have:

....

....

....

✓ Acquire:

....

....

....

Software

✓ Have:

....

....

....

(Continued)

✓ Acquire:

....

....

....

Office and organizational supplies

✓ Have:

....

....

....

✓ Acquire:

....

....

....

LEARN THE LEARNING MANAGEMENT SYSTEM AND/OR OTHER MEETING TOOLS

Prior to course start-up, try to find out what tools will be used, and familiarize yourself with them. Check out the university or course website to see whether an LMS is used. Blackboard, Canvas, Moodle, or Sakai are common higher education LMS brands. Google Classroom is more typically used with pre-college online learning. Some colleges and universities have proprietary systems customized to their institution. You will not be able to enter your course's classroom before the start date, but you can go to the LMS website and look for examples or tutorials.

Once you do have access, look around your online classroom. Click on all the links, check out the discussion board, chat function, assignments page, portfolio areas, grading rubrics and gradebook, the email system, and any other features.

If your class is not using an LMS, it might be more difficult to ascertain what technologies will be used. If you can get the syllabus, or communicate with the professor, look to see what platforms they will use. Open source or subscription-based options could include a videoconferencing space such as Zoom, Skype, Microsoft Teams, Adobe Connect, or Google Meet. There might also be a discussion platform such as Padlet. If you can try a demo or trial version and get acquainted with how the platforms work, the course will be less intimidating on day one.

It is to your advantage to learn how to navigate the LMS or other digital tools before you begin class. While they are designed to be user-friendly, nothing is more anxiety-producing than trying to learn how to do something or where to find something when you face a deadline.

 ## Learn the LMS or course technology scavenger hunt

How many of these items can you find in your LMS and/or other course tools?

'Human touch' such as friendly welcome message ☐

Syllabus ☐

Learning goals for the course ☐

Introduction or overview of the course ☐

Introduction or overview of a learning unit or module ☐

Recorded videos from your professor ☐

Contact information and contact protocols for reaching your professor ☐

Assignment requirements ☐

Assignment submission instructions ☐

(Continued)

Mobile app for accessing the course ☐

Scoring rubrics ☐

Criteria for marking assignments ☐

Gradebook ☐

Questions posted for discussion ☐

Discussion forum ☐

Forum or other place for informal chats with other students ☐

Videoconference link or app ☐

Explanation for how synchronous events will be handled ☐

Explanation for using tools or channels outside the LMS, such as: ☐

o   meeting platforms or videoconferencing links

o   shared folders

o   social media groups or hashtags

Links to library ☐

Links to articles or readings ☐

Links to media ☐

Links to other university services ☐

Tutorials for learning the LMS ☐

If the course is not in an LMS, was information about course requirements
and activities communicated? ☐

What is missing? ....

Who can you ask to find course materials you need? ....

BREATHE!

While you are gearing up with technology and preparations, and planning to manage your studies responsibly, remember that learning is meant to feed the soul as well as the mind. Plan breaks. Your mind might become numb, making it difficult to focus. Stepping away from the screen can be refreshing – and healthy! Make a cup of tea or coffee. Even a few minutes outside or a short walk will be revitalizing. Getting physical exercise will help your brain work! Sometimes you can find the way to phrase a sentence or the answer to a problem once you have taken your eyes off the computer.

The great advantage of online learning is flexibility. When you manage your time, remember to fit in time with friends and family. Pay attention to school/life balance, which will be good preparation for sanity in your future professional life.

 Self-care

Running, meditation, drawing, listening to music: what works for you? It takes real self-discipline to practise self-care when you are very busy.

Identify three steps you will take to avoid excessive stress this term:

1 ....

2 ....

3 ....

Sometimes a friend, in or out of school, can help you keep a balance. Who will you turn to when you need support or companionship during your online learning experience?

FINAL CHECKLIST: HOW TO KNOW YOU ARE DONE

I can identify the type of e-learning and platform for my course(s). ☐

I am confident I can succeed with synchronous or asynchronous communications and class activities. ☐

I am self-aware of learning styles and ways I process assignments, and am developing skills to fill any gaps. ☐

I know what to consider when communicating with my professor. ☐

I know how to analyse the syllabus and assignment descriptions to discern expectations and requirements. ☐

I am ready to critically read course textbooks and assigned readings. ☐

I can search and find relevant articles in the library or online. ☐

I am prepared to create written work, from short posts to lengthy papers. ☐

I am committed to creating original work and avoid plagiarism. ☐

I am equipped to work collaboratively with other learners to complete assignments. ☐

I am willing to participate in discussions. ☐

I am keen to treat the professor, any tutors or teaching assistants, and fellow learners with respect. ☐

I will look critically at assessment rubrics and follow any advice given as feedback on my work. ☐

I have the internet connection, hardware and software needed to be fully engaged in the class. ☐

I will manage my time and keep a study-life balance. ☐

I commit to making time for self-care and fun. ☐

MILESTONE

CONGRATULATIONS!

You have the mindset, self-awareness, skills and understanding needed to be a successful e-learner!

GLOSSARY

Academic engagement: Your level of engagement with your course. Online engagement is demonstrated by participation in official online forums, and the online media which is presented and intended as part of your course through the Learning Management System (LMS) or Virtual Learning Environment (VLE).

Academic integrity/honesty: This refers to honesty in your work. When you use the work or ideas of someone else you must give them the credit they deserve. Always cite and reference your sources to avoid committing plagiarism, which is punishable by loss of funding or possible expulsion.

Academic style: A system of formatting and referencing sources in academic writing. Common systems are APA, MLA, and Harvard.

Academic voice: How you construct and write your work for academic presentation. A formal way of writing and expressing reasons, points or arguments which includes supporting evidence.

Assignment: Assignments often require written work such as essays or research papers, but can also be a presentation, small-group work or team project. It will be a requirement of your course, will be given to you by your lecturer and used as an opportunity for them to assess and grade your progression on the course.

Asynchronous: Communication with an interval of time between message and response.

Bibliography: This is a list of every resource you have consulted in the creation of your assignment submission but not necessarily cited in it. An *annotated bibliography* includes a short description or summary of each sources.

Blended learning (also known as hybrid learning): Online and face-to-face learning are combined in a single course.

Citation: A notation for a quote or paraphrase from someone else's work, which shows where you have gained information and ideas. Citations are formatted in specific academic styles.

Collaborative e-learning: Students work together in response to an assignment, or to create a paper or project that represents all their contributions. (See **Team charter or agreement.**)

e-learning or online learning: All learning activities of the course occur online.

Learning Management System (LMS) (also known as Virtual Learning Environment [VLE]): This is a private website accessible only by registered students and faculty. Features allow for content and resources to be shared, and for discussions, assignment submission, communication within the class members, and rubrics and gradebooks.

Near synchronous: Communication with a short time-lag between message and response.

Reference list / references: This is the list at the end of your assignment of all of the books, articles, web pages or other sources you have cited in your writing. This must be presented in an appropriate academic style format.

Synchronicity: Communication with immediate response to messages; partners are online, on the same software platform, at the same time, with single focus on the communication or event.

Synchronous: Communication with immediate response to messages; communication partners are online, on the same software platform, at the same time.

Team charter or agreement: A statement or plan that spells out who does what on group or collaborative e-learning.

Videoconferencing (also known as web conferencing): Platforms that can be used for one-to-one or group communications. Videoconferencing allows communication partners to see each other and converse, or video chat, as well as for presenters to share content. Interactions can be verbal, visual, or in writing.

REFERENCES

Anderson, L., Bloom, B. S., Krathwohl, D. and Airasian, P. (2000). *Taxonomy for learning, teaching and assessing: A revision of Bloom's Taxonomy of Educational Objectives* (2nd ed.). New York: Allyn & Bacon, Inc.

Blackbourn, N. (2020). Digital note-taking. *Note-taking expert.* Retrieved from https://notetakingexpert.com/digital-note-taking/

Bloom, B., Engelhart, M., Furst, E., Hill, W. and Krathwohl, D. (1956). *Taxonomy of educational objectives: Book 1, Cognitive domain.* New York: David McKay and Company.

Fleming, N. D. and Mills, C. (1992). Not another inventory, Rather a catalyst for reflection. *To Improve the Academy, 11*(137–155).

Johnston, C. A. (2006). *Unlocking the will to process reflecting individual learning styles and learn.* Thousand Oaks: Corwin Press.

Katzenbach, J. R. and Smith, D. K. (2015). *The wisdom of teams.* New York: Harvard Business School.

Litt, E., Zhao, S., Kraut, R. and Burke, M. (2020). What are meaningful social interactions in today's media landscape? A cross-cultural survey. *Social Media + Society, 6*(3), 2056305120942888. doi:10.1177/2056305120942888

Salmons, J. (2019). *Learning to collaborate, collaborating to learn: Engaging students in the classroom and online.* Sterling: Stylus.

Šimonová, I., Poulová, P. and Bílek, M. (2011). *Learning styles within eLearning: didactic strategies.*

Šimonová, I., Poulová, P. and Kriz, P. (2020). *Personalization in eLearning: from Individualization to Flexibility.*

Wallace, M. and Wray, A. (2016). *Critical reading and writing for postgraduates.* London: SAGE Publications.

Zimmerman, B. J. (2000). Self-efficacy: An essential motive to learn. *Contemporary Educational Psychology 25*(1) doi.org/10.1006/ceps.1999.1016